For the LOVE of everything

Lisa Cairns

Transcribed and re-worded
to format live recordings of Lisa Cairns
into written form by Julie Rumbarger.

Chapters

Story	13
Juicy Drama	21
Bitter-Sweet	31
Aliveness	35
No Inside or Outside	39
Simplicity	45
Tough Story	49
Liberation	55
Love	59
Want	63
Comparison	67
Worth	71
Body	75
One-ness	79
Separation	81
Overlooked	83
Peace	85
Fading Game	89
Ecstatic	93
Dog	99

Questions and Answers

Love Affair	105
Positive Thinking	109
Home	111
Quite	115
Samskaras	121
Self-Inquiry	125
Thought	127
How Did This Happen?	129
Daily Living	135
Falling in Love	139
Rape	143
Source	149
Purpose	153
All You	155
Loss Program	161
What Can I Do?	165
Doer-ship	171
La-La Land	175
Reality	179
Conditioning	183

Irrelevant	187
One Flow	201
Other	207
Who Cares?	211
Money	213
Claiming	219
Loss	221
Grief	223
Death	225
Bliss	227
Greed	229
Banana Fritters	231
You Don't Have a Life	233

*Out beyond ideas of wrongdoing and rightdoing,
There is a field. I'll meet you there.*

*When the soul lies down in that grass,
The world is too full to talk about.
Ideas, language, even the phrase 'each other'
doesn't make any sense.*

Meveiana Jelaluddin Rumi. 13th Century.

Preface

We are so used to being convinced by intellectual ideas. We are so used to listening to something intellectually and understanding it intellectually and thinking "that's it." What I am talking about is not intellectual. It's not about me convincing you of something. It may sound like it.

What is being talked about here cannot be put into words in any way. This can't be made sense of.

This is talking about the mystery of *this*, of what is.

What *is*, is so incredibly mysterious, it's not something that you can ever understand. All the "person," or the mind, is used to looking at, is in intellectual understanding, and knowing this intellectually. It seems impossible to the mind that this is not about you getting something, or understanding something. All of the intellectually processed information that you have learned about in spirituality, all the books that have been read, are not it. Maybe they are pointing to something though. Maybe there is a resonance beyond the words.

This isn't about having a good argument or a good presentation in non-duality. This isn't about making sense. It is so simple and obvious that it is impossible for the intellect to understand. There can be a resonance that is beyond the words, a knowing beyond the intellect, but it's not thought or an understanding. It's not something "you" can know.

What this *is*, is entirely confusing to the intellect that is very busy in struggling to grasp onto something, anything. What I am pointing at here is the falling away of the one that is trying to hold on.

The "person," the "you," is something in time and in thought. This "person," this "you," is not who you are. Time arises *in* this, but "you" are not a product of time. Who you are, without the "you," is Aliveness, Being-ness. What *Is*. No-thing and every-thing.

It's not about a "you" in time. It's that Am-ness that is prior to that "you." You, the time-bound you, the character, arises *in* that. Alive-ness does not arise because of the character. The Alive-ness is right here. It's the stillness **and** the movement. You don't need to understand it. It's not about your understanding, or you getting it, or you seeing it, or you knowing it.

It is what *Is*. ~

Story

My memory is bad these days – so maybe I misremember things, and leave things out. Also, I want to point out this is only Lisa's version of events. It's not the truth, it's not what happened, but it's what's recorded in the Lisa brain. I am sure the others in the story would tell it completely differently.

The high board.

Often my parents would take us swimming in the local pools. I think on a Friday night or a Saturday afternoon. I think it was mostly my dad that would take us. I remember him being the shark chasing us, the joy of the game, his familiar face popping up from the water going 'Rarrrr.' Sweet.

I remember one of the pools had a high diving board. There were three, a small, middle, and a very high one.

My older brother James would run to the top one and jump straight away. I would follow him up and still be on the edge of the highest diving board on his second turn. I always wanted to follow him. I loved his courage. He seemed so brave to me.

Sometimes I would sit the whole of the swimming session at the top of the high diving board waiting to jump, my feet dangling over the edge. Often, as my dad called me in, I would start crying as I climbed back down the steps. I never wanted to be afraid of anything.

My brother.

My brother was a beautiful child. People thought he was a girl, he was so pretty. He had deep red ringlets – large hazel eyes and his personality was soft and giggly.

He was born three years before me.

I don't really remember too much from our childhood, it feels so distant now, like a different life. There are points that stand out, sometimes, the bits that shocked me, or frightened me, rather than the good memories. Shame that's what the brain records but it's pretty obvious that's how it would work.

I think the saddest memories this body has witnessed have been watching my brother.

I was ten when my brother was first put in a psychiatric ward. He was thirteen. The explanation that had been given to me was that he had broken his head; like a broken arm, but his head was broken. I noticed if I told people this they would look at me with sad eyes and ask me if I was okay. I didn't really understand this. I didn't understand it was bad or sad. I didn't understand that this broken head was what made him scream for hours in the night with my dad having to pin him down. I didn't understand his broken head was what made him shake with fear in refusing to eat, or have him make my gran and I wear tin foil to protect us against aliens. I thought that was just my brother. I wasn't really sure what a broken head was. I quite liked breaking my arm; I got loads of attention and presents. It hurt at first, but it made me feel important. So I wasn't sure that it was such a bad thing.

I didn't realize it was BAD until we left him for the first time in the hospital. The nurses had to restrain him as he screamed and begged us not to leave. I found this rather amusing, so much activity and shouting, like the TV, like *EastEnders*. My mother, Father, I and my dog had to walk down a thin path to leave – him screaming and banging on the glass door behind us – nurses everywhere. I hear my dad laugh – thank god, I thought, it's okay to laugh. So I laughed and laughed. My mum in front of me cries, wails, like she was being killed. How odd. I went to her and I say 'don't cry Mum – it's funny really - Dad is laughing,' she looks like she is going to collapse and my dad rushes forward and catches her. I look at his face. He wasn't laughing, I realized. He was crying.

The guilt.

I had never in my ten years experienced the agony of guilt. I felt physically sick for weeks.

My parents had cried on the way home that night in the car. I sat in the back with my dog Bonny and burned in guilt. I thought it was funny. I thought it was a joke. But it wasn't. I had never seen them both cry before. I didn't know my dad did. And I had said to them out loud that it was funny.

I couldn't play with my friends at school. I couldn't concentrate. My insides ached and I just kept replaying the hour-long journey with them crying. I now knew my brother's broken head was *very* BAD.

I cried myself to sleep at night, so sad at them being sad. I wished I could take all their pain away. I cried and cried at the sadness of them. My parents looked so sad all the time. My mum would cry in the morning as she did her hair.

I began to dream of ways I could help people. I dreamed of setting up a dog home to rescue unwanted dogs. Funny what the mind does when there is pain.

One night I plucked up the courage to apologize to my mum for laughing. We were watching *EastEnders* and it just came out. I tried to explain to her that I didn't understand it was bad. She hugged me and told me it was all right. The guilt began to fade after this.

It never really ended, my brother's illness (well, that's what they call it). It's been 25 years now of drugs and doctors and social workers and hospitals. I can tell you the saddest tales of suffering. Suffering beyond anyone's imagination. Not because there was a problem in the flow, but because my brother's brain imagined problems.

Hours sitting outside the hospital, in the car, crying, just for the sadness of him, of knowing no matter what happened, it wouldn't make his brain tell better stories.

I saw hell wasn't about the flow; it wasn't about what happened, it was about how the brain interpreted it. Even though society would tell you it was about the flow I knew it wasn't; my brother saw hell when it wasn't there.

My life began to get darker after that day.

My parents were heart broken, and they seemed to spend less and less time at home, of course. My disabled gran lived with us – so I was often left with her.

There were good times – there were friends, and boys, and laughter, holidays, animals, but I was left alone more and more with my brother after he came out of hospital.

Because my gran was disabled and we had a big house she was often in the front of the house, and my brother and I were in the back.

Naturally, we began to act out really weird behaviours together. We argued a lot and physically fought. I use to feel so powerless around him.

I began to make myself sick in secret. It was such a great release, that sounds odd, but a lot of the time, to a bulimic, the purging is the best part. It grew and grew until I was binging and purging sometimes ten to fifteen times a day.

I didn't purposely choose to become a spiritual seeker, in a way I had to, otherwise I was more than likely going to die young from the bulimia. But that wasn't the real spur, actually the question WHY? was what got it going, why THIS? I was still in my teens and basically I HAD to find answers, there was no way this bundle of energy could have settled with marrying and children, or even doing the rat race. I had to know WHY.

For ten years it felt like I was stripped of everything that I thought I knew. It felt like I was constantly sitting on the edge of the diving board. I can't really tell you how or why it happened, it just happened like that. At points it was very physically painful. Everything was being lost and everything was questioned and at points it was very exciting. There was reading of books, listening to speakers, practicing weird practices and living with bodies that were mostly empty of self. There were drugs, sex, booze, food, shitting and life, just life, which was in a constant momentum of change.

I never knew the way. There was always doubt. I never thought that this was the way to freedom. It happened without me knowing it was happening.

Then one day, after many experiences and awakenings, everything changed. It didn't suddenly make sense, it didn't suddenly click and there was an understanding.

There was just LOVE. Everywhere, the boundless intimacy of everything but not for Lisa ...... it was everything.

One day I was inside the body, relating to the world through time and "me," then one day that was gone and there was *everything*. The Aliveness was no longer Lisa's and bound inside a body. It didn't belong to a story in time, or a description in words, or a body moving through the world. It was every-thing and no-thing and completely 'What the Hell!'

It wasn't knowable.

And this isn't some final state. In this weird reality where this world is seemingly experiencing through a body, the body is changing and developing, and change and growth and realizations still carry on. I don't see myself as liberated or un-liberated, there or not there, finished or not finished. I don't know where I am. I would need to know YOU in order to judge myself and I don't ;).

So now there is talking and writing about this, but there is no idea of a path or a way **to** this. All of it seems like a dream now, me, and my life and the way through time, a dream to nowhere.

Talking and listening is happening, but what is spoken of, or written about, is not known by a someone. It can't even be known that Lisa lost everything. What a cosmic joke.

And then, we laugh. -

Juicy Drama

Beginning somewhere around the age of two or three, sometimes younger, we start assuming that we are separate from everything and everyone, and that we are acting out our own apparent life.

We are told, by our parents and society, that we have to make the right choices, and that it's our responsibility to lead and live a good life. We are often reminded by our parents that we need to plan, and know what it is that we are going to be or do when we grow up. There is constant reinforcement of this idea of choice, and that we are a separate entity, or person that can choose.

There is nothing wrong or right about this belief, it's just what seems to have happened through evolution. With this belief in separation, however, suffering arises.

There can be fun in the apparent choice making, but for the most part it brings suffering.

Suffering happens when the mind becomes fixated and obsessed in making the "right" decision to ensure its happiness in the future. Take, for example, the simple choice of what kind of cake to buy at the grocery store. If you choose the wrong cake you might then have five minutes of a really bad cake. If we consider the larger choices like a house, boyfriend or girlfriend, children, dog or career, you can imagine the pressure in choosing correctly.

While this is happening inwardly, it is also going on externally, in blame with others who we believe have chosen wrongly and chosen to hurt me. This game of "my choice/their choice" is cause for much suffering; this idea that I am a separate person, they are a separate person, acting separately and choosing, and I, or they, are wrong or right. Most of the arguments with your family, lover or friends are about choice, that one simple idea that says, 'I am separate from everything else and I choose.'

But, is it true? Are you sure that you are the choice maker?

Are you separate from everything, and are you acting and choosing independently?

If we take nature into consideration and imagine a tree, we know that the tree does not choose to grow or not grow. We're quite happy with the idea that the tree just grows. We're content as well with the wind when it blows. It doesn't choose to blow, it just blows. Rarely do we get angry at the wind.

The same is true with the birds and dogs and animals. Most of the time we assume they are not in control of things and that they do as they do, and we don't think that much about them. But the human spends so much time thinking of how we will choose and how they will choose.

It's easy to conclude that we don't choose how the body works: We haven't had a choice in our looks, because that's genetic. If we take a look at our talents, maybe there is some apparent choice, but most of it is inherited. We didn't choose the colour of our skin or how much our hair grows. We didn't choose our gender, but we think we *do* choose action? We *do* choose our own action and we are separate from everything else? We act separately and that choice of action is totally independent of everything else? Is it really true? *Mine. Me.* 'I am choosing freely in every moment.' That's the assumption in nearly all humans.

Let's say, for instance, that someone says something rude to you and shouts loudly. The thoughts might come that they acted independently from everything else and that they shouldn't have done this, they should have acted differently. Even more thoughts might come about what it did to you, and why do people treat you this way, 'Why is life not fair?'

Then the thoughts might spend hours blaming this person for what they should and shouldn't have done, rather than 'that's just the way it is,' and the actions are merely coming and going, like the tree grows or the bird sings. All of these stories get stuck in time, me/you, separation and free will.

But how can anything be separate from anything else? How can one action be separate from everything that came before it? We assume that we have independent choice in this moment and that we are separate entities who are choosing. How is it that we separate out our actions?

Where does a choice start and where does a choice stop? Did choice start when your parents met? Did choice start when you woke up in a bad mood that morning, or with how well you did at school or on that perfectly chosen career path? Was it when you were late because of traffic, or when you broke your arm at the age of ten? Did your choosing start when you couldn't say no to that whole pack of cookies, or was it when your parents died, or a bird shat on your head?

When did you begin to have choice?

In the flow of things, where does anything start or stop, including choice? Is the tree separate from the earth, the sunlight from the water? Is a choice separate from its environment, and everything that came before, and will possibly show up in the future?

You think so!

You have seemingly had years of blaming yourself and others for messing it all up. But I'll bet you've not been too shy in taking credit for any experience when you thought it went well.

Me. Me. Me. *Who?*

All of this worry about your choices – career and what your partner is going to do, or what will happen to your kids – is all based on the idea that you are a separate entity and you have independent action.

I am going to make a bold statement that many people will want to reject: *There has never been an independent entity choosing anything.*

It's all been an absolute lie, a fantasy; a fantasy with great highs and great lows. "You" was based on an assumption, in a made up language, that has become an energetic expression of "me" inside the body, separate from all the things out "there."

This has been the trick of the human, to dream that it is separate. This is where all the mental illness, unhappiness and suffering come from. There has never been a you in the body that is separate from all other things.

It is all one energy expressing itself.

A common question asked is, 'Why has this happened to the human?' Language seems to be a big part of it, and the fact that we can comprehend time. We have taken language to be a truth, not just a description of what's happening, and we've taken our self as something found in that language. We've been taught that our nature is something that is describable, when it's actually indescribable.

It might sound a bit odd if you have never heard this subject before, but describing is actually arising *in* your nature. Your nature is prior to the description of it. Therefore, you cannot describe yourself, but we are convinced that we can. All that we can describe is actions, and the body, and what the body does.

We are convinced that we can describe ourselves. What we are describing is just the body, which is seemingly moving through time. That's not actually who you are.

That is the mistake.

There is something here that was there before the body, and is there no matter how much the body changes, whether you think of yourself as a good person or bad person, two years old or ninety years old, even if you have had brain damage and your actions and appearance have really changed. Life could have turned someone that was once really friendly into someone that is now grumpy, and yet that original Alive-ness has never changed. We can all relate to this when we have that feeling of not being aware of our age. That's because only the body ages, not the original Being-ness. Your essence is not dependent on the body.

The body arises *in* your essence and so does everything else.

As soon as I use the word "I", you may think that I am meaning something in time. What I am referring to is something that is timeless, still, and is no-thing, but is also every-thing.

When the obsession with choosing begins to loosen from being in a contracted sense of a separate self, it will begin to be seen, by no-one, that the nature of being is absolutely free and not bound to anything at all, yet it is everything.

Our essence has always been free, and suffering was only ever a dream that was never really even happening.

What this message is pointing to is what is actually happening, not what you "think" is happening. I can assure you that the thoughts have led you big-time astray. The obsession with choice has been a huge dream. What a good old juicy drama. ~

There is not a controller, because the controller has the same nature as the controlled. It is the subject which maintains the object. But when the subject is no longer relative, when it becomes the ultimate subject, then there is no more fuel for the object, and there is a fusion between the observer and the observed. It is the controller which maintains the object.

~ Jean Klein

Bitter-Sweet

Everything is being lost. The reading of these words, the light, the sounds from outside, the images; it's all continuously being lost. It appears and disappears.

It appears and disappears.

Without logic and complicated thinking, it appears from nowhere and disappears back to nowhere. It's all an absolute mystery.

Life is in a perpetual state of loss where everything is going, going, going. Though as soon as you look at everything again, it is always fresh and not what you had seen before. It's always brand new.

The human has the ability to think in a complicated way and to see in time. It has become identified with complicated thinking by believing that it has, and is, the body, and it has, and is, the controller, and **it** moves the body through time. In this complicated thinking, it dreams it is an entity that is separate from other things, and that it can obtain other things. This bitter-sweet drama acts out because it seems it can get the lover, and get the money, and get to travel on the airplane. But if we stand back and have a greater and more expanded look, it's also continuously being lost, and the human wants to cover that bit up!

It wants to hold on to all the things that it loves so dearly: the mother, the father, the kids, the lover, the home and the money. It can't. Everything is going. As soon as it appears, it is changing and it is moving.

This is all *one* energy, all one expression of nothing-ness. The human will never find a fixed place. Never.

That's the drama of the human. The ability to think and have complicated thinking has made for a very bitter-sweet life that is full of great highs and extreme lows. Just when you think you've got it figured out, it's wonderful...but, like everything else, it will go.

Everything you love so dearly will go. That's the nature of life; it's in a constant state of movement.

However life never abandons itself for as soon as one thing goes another thing appears, this is total love.
LOST = LOVE.

Aliveness

There is this Alive-ness, or consciousness, and this Alive-ness has been there the whole time. This Alive-ness is always here. It is here in moments of great happiness and great sorrow, pain and indifference, when drugs have been taken or in sitting on the toilet.

This Aliveness has always been here. What comes and goes *in aliveness* is 'I am a body,' 'I am a thought', 'I am an idea,' 'I am upset', 'I am angry,' 'I am a drug addict,' or 'I am peaceful.'

There is nothing wrong with any of it. It's all appearing and disappearing. But the Alive-ness never disappears. It's always *Alive*.

Aliveness is prior to 'I am the body.' It does not start or stop anywhere but the thoughts will say that Alive-ness is inside the body. The thoughts will say that this *Aliveness* is inside the body and that it is because the body is alive. But, it is actually the other way around.

The body is what comes and goes inside of this *Alive-ness*. *Aliveness* is number one, or first and its not referring to the life or death of a thing. (Although there never really is death, just change)

The most wonderful part of this *Alive-*ness is that you will never be able to find it or see it, or know it in thoughts or in any intellectual way.

Yet everything IS *Alive-*ness.

Everything is that *Aliveness* prior to 'I am the body' and all the thoughts. There actually aren't other things, because it's all *Alive-*ness. It's all One thing. All "things" are moving; therefore, there are no things. Everything appears in *Alive-*ness as *one* movement.

The mind though, is splitting up things and saying 'I am a body,' and 'they are separate from me.' That apparent separation has created this 'I am separate, and I am not good enough, and I am vulnerable.'

There is nothing wrong with a description of the bodies or the seeming things (which are always moving so they are no-thing). There's nothing wrong with that, but it's **not** who you are. It's not a truth in any way. It's a description that has appeared. But a seeming separate entity has claimed the description and got lost in it.

This description may sound quite complicated, but it's actually just pointing back to what *is,* and it's really simple.

This reading is a very simple pointing back to what is actually happening. It's not complicated thinking or exclusive. It's pointing back to the nature of what *Is.* The beauty of it all is that you **are** that Alive-ness.

What can happen is that the energy can change from this very narrow place of "me and my limitation" to *everything,* which is boundlessness. It's the collapse of everything you think you know and take as a reality. What is actually happening is *Oneness.*

Is there anything outside of that? -

*The choice-less Truth of who you are is revealed
to be permanently here permeating everything.
Not a thing and not separate from anything.*

~ Gangaji

No Inside or Outside

What seemingly happens is the baby is born, and the baby has no sense that it was born, or that it is a baby, or that it is separate from life or its mother. There is no complicated thinking in any way, no energetic contraction of inside and outside. The baby has no sense of cot or hand or stop or start, no sense that "I" have begun two months ago, or that I am a boy or a girl. There is pure *Aliveness* happening, everywhere.

What begins to happen is a beginning of a recognition that says, 'I am a body' or 'I finish at the end of my body and my mother is out there.' It starts as an energetic feeling rather than a thought. Babies cannot rationally think, but there does seem to be a growing sense of 'I am a person' or 'I am John.'

The first conditioning begins after the name is established and soon thereafter the child is taught by the parents about what is good and what is bad. This is the beginning of the reward system conditioning, this particular conditioning being the most important, in that it says you've got to do good and you have got to choose good actions. There are some exceptions that can be different and the child may be conditioned to do bad. This bad behaviour is regarded as positive; therefore the child will get attention by being bad.

None of this is wrong or right, it's simply something that is appearing, which is no different from the light or trees. It's just another form of life expressing itself. What then carries on is the child meets more children, and the conditioning about being a good child and playing nicely with your friends happens. Children learn that they have to be nice in order to be rewarded or behave badly and receive bad attention.

Soon enough, they move into school, and learn to write all of these letters, and think in a logical way in order to get rewarded. At this point in the human's life, it is not yet suffering. It may be a bit uncomfortable at times, but mostly there is just *Boundlessness*, and the child does not have too much identity. Gradually the child begins to compete and it begins to want to be the best because the conditioning teaches that getting the most attention is personal happiness and fulfilment, though some children might push away personal attention, because they may have a specific conditioning on what fulfilment means to them.

Puberty comes, and fulfilment is found in getting the opposite sex's attention or in planning for the future. More and more these concepts grow, and less and less this, or what *Is*, is important. Importance is found in the seeking in time. What is actually happening is third-best, really. The first-best is future, the-second best is past and the third-best is this. "*This*" really isn't very exciting anymore, because the excitement comes from longing for the future, or what you're going to get in the future, when you become rich, or get a house, or do certain things.

Seeking continues, and keeps on growing. Now, he or she might be going to University, or finishing University and getting married, or getting a home, or getting a dog, or traveling the world. All of this in the pursuit of ones own personal happiness.

There is nothing wrong with this game. This game is something that appears.

It's not in your control; it's not in anyone's control. It's not that parents should stop conditioning their children or never teach them anything. It's just what seems to appear in the human dynamic, this huge focus on time. The focus is that you are a somebody in time, and you must strive for your own happiness. And *this* is hardly even talked about or noticed.

The first time that I began to hear this was in Buddhism, where they would say that you've got to be in the moment. There was a resonating with that. I knew that there was something here that was not quite right about longing or grasping for the future. It began to become obvious that the longing was often because I felt uncomfortable or I felt not enough. I began listening to other speakers, and it became evident that I could not make myself be in the moment, because that would be a thought, or just another idea, and that idea began to get eaten up or deconstructed.

There was a process that apparently took place, and all of this craving and grasping for future events in order to bring happiness began to crumble. They crumbled through the getting of the things sometimes, and then it was, 'Ah, now what?' I would go on this super holiday and travel for six months, and yet it was still life, and there was still discomfort or disappointment or sadness arising. Maybe I would "get" the boyfriend that I had been chasing for two years, and the conclusion may have been that it was more pleasurable to experience the longing for him.

It became more and more obvious that the whole of life, or the motivation of life, had been based on striving for the future. It was never about what was happening right now, it was more about this huge strategy of what will be. What was actually wanted was right now, and that was ignored. If there was tiredness, that was covered up with 'No, I must work to be successful.' If there was hunger that would be covered with 'No, I must not eat, to be slim.' If I was with my lover it was more about trying to impress them, and keep them happy so that "I" could "get" and keep their love. I was never actually just *Being*. I was always in a strategy for the future.

What is actually wanted in the moment has all of these layers on top of it, these layers of having to "do" something in order to actually do what you want. It's like an action appears and has to fit into this whole strategy of "getting this fulfilment someday."

It may become more and more obvious that you are never going to get fulfilled. Getting fulfilled in the future is dreaming, a dreamland, an absolute false reality of this imagined pleasure or imagined "you" that will get there.

We can't even answer the question of who we are, let alone what this pleasure could possibly be. What is this pleasure that is going to be so fulfilling?

I asked a young man once, who was very interested in sex, if he would want a constant orgasm. He sat there and really thought about it, 'No, I wouldn't want that. Just a couple of hours, maybe.'

This dream feels so real, but really, *what is this ultimate pleasure that we are going to get?*

There are all of these "ifs" happening. The "if-only's." It can be so alluring, and it seems like the most real thing, that if I do this for another, I will be happy. If I just sacrifice this, I will be happy. If I just stop this, I will be happy. If I make my parents respect me, I will be happy. If I do well enough at work, people will appreciate me. If I get enough money, I can stop worrying about money. If I can get him or her to recognize me, then I will be happy. I will be happy when he stops creating the problem. He is the problem. If I can get him to stop creating the problem, I will be happy.

It goes on and on. ~

Simplicity

How to communicate this? How to tell you or speak about this *being* it, or this *being* what was always wanted? The reading of this, ***this is it***, baby, and it's never going to **not** be *this*.

The person spends all its time in wanting something else and thinking about something else, or trying to get to something else, or trying to DO something else – and it can't. This is what is happening, and it's all right!

This is enough. You don't need all of those fancy things that you think you do. There is nothing wrong with moving towards fancy things, but it's not in the finality of getting the fancy things. It's the moving toward. It is whatever is happening. If there is a working towards getting a house, then it's in the actual working towards it, not the getting. It's always about what is happening.

The mind plays these games of, 'No, this is better. Why is this happening? I don't want this. I should have something better. It can't be cutting the carrots. It can't be stroking the dog. It can't be my mundane job. It can't be lack of money.' All of that is conceptual and in an untrue reality.

All of these problems arise with the idea that you are a someone separate inside of a body. If that was not there, all of these problems would not arise. This idea that you are acting independently from everything else is not true.

You might then ask who it is that I am talking to? Why is she writing this? Who is she speaking to? It all begins to get really odd. I can't answer that for you.

This is just coming back to the simplicity of Being, even though it was never really lost. Just Being. The Being-ness and Alive-ness, which is always here and never changes, and isn't separate from anything, and never suffered.

It dreamed of suffering, and a someone that messed up their life or messed up their relationship, that hurt others and got hurt, and did wrong and did right. It dreams of that, and for some reason the Lisa body is pointing out that that is not true.

There really has never been a going home, because there has always been that Being-ness, dreaming and playing all of these different things. It's like the light of a film, which projects the film. All the film is light and in the film there is drama, but it's not affecting the light, and yet it is the light. The light is not suffering, yet it is playing suffering.

What **can** happen is the contracted personal energy of the characters in the film expands back to the light – yet the film and the bodies carry on doing the same thing, but they are no longer the characters appearing in them.

There can be the collapse of the dream that you're separate from the light. Alive-ness, the original I, The Big I, Being-ness, Consciousness, Light, whatever you want to call it, is *Free*. It is boundless, and it cannot be limited to the body. It is not inside or outside. It cannot be found and yet it *IS* everything. "I" is everywhere. It plays this funky game that is not really happening, of dreaming that "I" is inside a body and in relationships with other "I's" inside of bodies.

There is something that is so boundless and huge. I am talking about what is when this energy or tight contracted self collapses. I don't know how or why it collapses, and I also don't know why it even started, it just kind of falls away, and that dream that you were separate dies. With that, the suffering dies as well.

Ultimately that collapse is going to happen in physical death, but it can seem to happen when the body is alive as well: the death of the energy that is claiming to be certain things over others. After that, the character still carries on, along with the characteristics of the body. The one that took that to be "who" it was fell away, and the character continues to be another thing arising *IN* this. It is no longer "you" but a part of *this*. ~

Tough Story

No freedom is found in morality. No freedom is found in worrying. No freedom is found in trying to save things. The daydream that all of those things will make your life better is a lie. The body might be saving bodies or animals and the body might be planning, but the idea that that will make you better is a lie. The freedom is in the *act* of what is happening.

Most people have tough stories. The rape victim wants to feel like theirs is the worst story, but most people I have met have had bad stories. Most people want to tell me their bad stories. This is a life of pleasure and pain. Most people have had tragedy and trauma and discomfort, and I am saying that the freedom is right here and right now. It is not found in sorting it out in time.

Life is so messy and brutal and bloody and beautiful and divine and pretty. Love is the end of that one that is trying to get out of it. It's so crazy that the freedom is *in* the rape, not trying to avoid the rape. I am not saying that the body doesn't fight. That's not what's being talked about. It's the end of that seeking energy. The freedom is in the moment *of b*eing raped and brutalized. It's horrific and awful, and I am not denying that. It's bloody and painful and brutal, but the freedom is in the sensation of it, not trying to get away in dreamland. That is not saying that the body doesn't fight like hell, more than likely the body will.

Right here there is absolute freedom, always, in death, brutality, murder and rape.

That is what is being pointed to in this radical and beautiful message. You don't have to be rich, you don't have to have a privileged life, and you don't have to have a good background, a bad background, a successful background or unsuccessful background in order for this to be heard. You don't have to be clever, good or bad. The freedom is right here.

Animals and birds are singing it. Watch.

Animals have it very tough physically, but the human has it a lot tougher because they have a dream that it is happening **to** them, and that they are a somebody in time. Most probably every time you eat, an animal is seemingly being tortured.

Let's be honest, most meat that people eat is about cheapness, not about fairness in the flow of things. Animals have it very tough physically, but if you watch them, there is absolute freedom there. There is pain happening, but there is not this energy that is trying to get out of it. The body may be trying to move away from it, but there is not this dreaming in time that says 'This shouldn't be happening to me! Why is this happening to me? Are they going to murder and kill me? What am I going tell my parents or my loved one, my partner?'

This is so brutal and comical that a white girl, nicely presented, has to speak this.

In a way, it may be that a guy could not get away with speaking this message; it may sound much too terrible. That's the beauty of non-duality, so many pointers without one of them being right. They can't ever be right. There can be a pointing in the most horrific situation, and it can be heard, this freedom.

It's everywhere, *in* everything. It is divine and it never leaves you. Everything else comes and goes but this Aliveness, this silence and movement, this silence and sound is free. The Alive-ness, the Being-ness is always here. Whether the plane is crashing or the child is being raped, it is always here.

The message that is coming out of this mouth refuses to let you off the hook by giving you a false hope story, giving you a story of peace in the flow of life. The story of, 'If you follow this, this non-duality, then we will find a more peaceful world in the future. This message will bring a peaceful society.' Forget that. Hitler said that, the politicians and religious speakers say that.

Most of the teachings in non-duality say that if you follow what they are saying, it will create a more peaceful future. I'm not going to give you that story in order to make this more bearable to hear. We don't know the future. We know only *this* and there is one freedom here and it is no~thing and every~thing.

If you want someone to promise you a good land, a better future, a more peaceful earth, then go to politics, go to Hitler. Hitler promised a much better earth in the future. Go follow your prime ministers, the political leaders or the spiritual leaders that promise, 'This movement, this message, is going to produce a peaceful world.'

I don't know.

It may be that this message will produce a more helpful world, but that is not the freedom. Dreaming of peace in the world is **not** the freedom. The freedom is the collapse of the dreaming, and then *this* is what is. *This* comes back to life and what is actually happening rather than seeing through this foggy distant dreaming veil.

This message may produce a strong reaction, in fact it often does. That is because people are afraid, which is understandable. There may be a desire to control or hold on to a more peaceful world. Really what is happening is, 'I'm scared and I can't bear this being out of control. I can't bear not hoping that I will control this and make this a better tomorrow.'

This is not controllable. It's absolutely wild. Physical death of the body could come at any moment. Right now, right here, in a way this is *absolute death*. Right here, a part of this isn't even happening, and another part of this is that *everything* is happening.

In the story of the Lisa dream, Lisa was addicted to doing good, being compassionate and saving the world. Basically, Lisa was petrified of fear and violence. That's all it is, really. I'm sorry to say that. It's such a romantic idea, "a peaceful future," and an idea that is based on fear.

This is the silence in which the words are arising from. *This* is the emptiness in which it all comes from and **is**.

It's okay if you want to keep dreaming that this message might be wrong, but no message is right. You're not going to find a right message. You're not even going to find a wrong message. Both of those are intellectual. This is talking about a dropping away of that energy that dreams of control, and it can never be put in the positive. ~

Liberation

What do you think liberation is? Most people think that it is pleasure, and they imagine themselves getting to a pleasure or a heaven in the future. There is also an imagination of eliminating pain as well as experiencing rewards.

What this *is*, is absolute death. The reward won't be there anymore. There will just be what is and what is happening. There won't be a **you** there that is happy that "you" got to liberation. It's **that** functioning that will have gone. There will be nothing to look for anymore to complete yourself.

That is what the person or "me" spends most of its time thinking about. That game of the person looking for completion in reading all the spiritual books, or planning to have kids, or planning to go traveling, **goes**. It's not that actions don't happen, but there is no sense anymore in looking for something more than what is happening, because there is not anybody there anymore to complete.

Thoughts still appear, the movements towards pleasure happen but everything is appearing in Boundlessness. It's not appearing **for** anyone anymore. That person that grew up in Mexico or England or Africa isn't experiencing what is anymore. There is just what *is*.

If the "me" could comprehend this, it wouldn't want it. This is the death of "you." This is the death of that one that was in love with trying to find love. The apparent "one" that is trying to get love is actually in love with the game of hide-and-seek. You might be reading this and be thinking, 'No, I'm not in love with it, she doesn't know what she is saying!' I assure you, the "me" is absolutely in love with it, and it is pissed off when it doesn't get it, very pissed off. That "not" getting it is part of the game of getting it.

Haven't you ever noticed that when you get someone in a relationship, you begin to lose interest? It's the chase that the "me" loves. When you feel you get them, you don't want them anymore. It's the same with everything else. When you feel you've got it, you don't want it anymore. It will be on to the next thing. Sometimes relationships can go on for years and you don't feel you've got them. So there is still that trying to impress them, and trying to get them.

This is the end of that game. That game has been a funky, fun and devastating experience. That person that was born 20, 30, 40 years ago, that went to school and had all of these experiences, and travelled the world and met lots of teachers, will **not** experience liberation.

That person dies, and then talking about the body or the character is just a practical or fun communication, in the moment, for practical or social matters. There will no longer be that "you" taking the descriptions of the body as who you are and living through that veil.

What is left is what is happening. The "me" hears this, and it longs for it. But it is not really longing for it. What it is looking for is the carrying on of the looking. It does not want the looking to end. It wants to look, look, and look some more, to work really hard and travel the world and get the promotion or get something in the future.

What is left when that person dies? What *is*. Which is the drinking of the tea, the light, the sounds, the smells. Liberation doesn't make the body a perfect body, or a hero, or special. It's just the absence of what I would call suffering.

What it *is*, is absolute emptiness and fullness at the same time. A huge void and silence that is empty, and not lonely but alone. The me has no clue about this emptiness. As that person collapses, this becomes absolute alone-ness. There is nobody left anymore.

If there is no you, there is no other.

Is this really what you want? You will only get what you want.

What will the body do without looking for liberation? It will be happy. There is no more journeying because there is no more leaving home.

This is it. This is it!

It has no purpose and it is going absolutely nowhere! Forms are appearing and disappearing for no reason at all. You are not going to get understanding, meaning, reason or heaven. The collapse of all of that will happen, and then there is just *this*. This is loss, not a getting or becoming. *This* is losing. ~

Love

All there *is*, is love. Even the act of personal love, that thinks and wishes and hopes and longs for love, is love. The burping and the taste of the dinner is love. Everything is love, but love is very much in motion.

Most people associate love with the high pleasures of falling in love with this other person. This personal love can carry a huge dramatic story like running into the sunset, holding hands and making love on the beach. It's a huge pleasure that most people associate with the heart area or a feeling in the chest. That is not what I mean when I say love.

There are two types of love. There is personal, relationship love and impersonal love.

Personal love is when love is personalized in two body-mind mechanisms; coming together with two dreams of falling in love and committing themselves to staying together for the next thirty years and keeping each other. This type of love is conditional. This is when there are two people needing things and requiring things and seeing the other in a time-bound reality. This type of love can have a lot of suffering and a lot of highs.

There is a lot of suffering because its foundation is that there is a separate entity in this other body, and they have free will and choice, and they have the ability to give this high pleasure of love. When they don't give me this love, they upset me, and I hate them. When they take it away it's because I have not done the washing up, or because there was a looking at another girl or another guy. This love will have arguments and rage about what the other person has chosen to do to me, or to hurt me, or let me down. Questions like 'Why are they not giving me my pleasures?' often arise in this type of love. They live in a dreamland.

Impersonal love is when there is a relationship that is without relationship. Two body-mind mechanisms are together, but they are, simply put, just together. There can be kissing and loving each other happening, but they are not kissing in time. They are just together, in this. They may even be together for ten years, kissing and touching, but they are always now and present. This kind of relationship is never about two people who are separate entities that have fallen in love and can choose to be together. ~

Want

More than likely what is wanted is a guide to constant pleasure. What is being looked for is a more pleasurable life, and more pleasurable sensations than painful, less irritation and conflict with others. That's more than likely what is wanted, which isn't wrong, but it **is** impossible.

Each body is caged to that specific story, or to those specific genes and conditioning, that specific life and circumstance. In a way, the body is a cage and it has to live out what it is. God knows what it is, but it's all spontaneously living out now. There is not a somebody inside the body that is in control of that.

Some bodies might have more pleasure, money and success and a lot of people around them worshiping them, while other bodies might have a poor, sick and painful life that is about fighting for survival. Some body-minds might have a nice life, but a very difficult conditioning, while others might have terrible lives and a very simple and easy conditioning.

There are many spiritual teachings that emphasize changing and improving the life circumstance by emptying yourself of conditioning, or not resisting life and "doing" something about changing that life. That is not what I am saying.

I am pointing to the *absence* of that self. It isn't about continuous pleasure or a continued state. It's about the absence of that lie. When that lie goes, it is just life as it is, and it is no longer a struggle anymore for a somebody. There may be difficult events that arise or pleasurable events, but there is no longer anybody inside the body anymore. There is just life happening, and the character appearing when the character needs to appear. But it is no longer living "through" that character anymore.

If you knew what I was talking about, you wouldn't want this. What you want, even though you can't possibly know it, is a more pleasurable life. You wouldn't want the end of you.

It's not at all like how you imagine. It's full-on living and there is no escape. The "me" is always escaping and dreaming, and making up better stories, and retelling the story to make it sound better. This is the absence of that person, the absence of the middleman.

It's full-on touching the computer and full-on touching the radiator. It's full-on coldness or hotness or happiness or sadness. It's full-on experiencing without a barrier anymore. The difference is that there isn't anybody that cares about it anymore in order to be happy. There isn't anyone who needs a certain experience.

It's absolute freedom, but not in any way that you can imagine.

You're not going to suddenly understand something, and get something, and then be able to express it to other people. You **lose** everything. You're not going to suddenly be better than everyone else because you're enlightened, because you're *gone*. You're not better or worse.

You're not going to care about saving the world anymore. You're not living in an imagination of what "should" be anymore. That doesn't mean that in seeing people hurting, the body doesn't respond and help. But it's no longer living in imagination. It doesn't mean that you won't give to charity, but you're not saving the world anymore. This is full-on.

You will most probably re-interpret what I'm saying to make it more bearable, especially the part about saving the world. This body-mind mechanism is such a little monkey. It likes to really say things full-on so that we're not beating around the bush or trying to put it nicely. ~

Comparison

In order to know yourself, you have to know another. All language works on the idea of comparison. I am this and you are that, I know this and you know that. This is big, this is small, and this is good, this is bad. If you have two kids, one might seem like it has better behaviour than the other one, so that is the good kid and the other one is the bad kid. Then you can add another child into the mix who is even better than both of them. Suddenly the good child is not good anymore, just average, and the bad kid is really bad.

It's all in comparison. We know colour by comparison, because if it was all just yellow there would be nothing. We know yellow because of all the other shades. We know who we think we are the exact same way. If who we think we are is always in comparison with other objects, then that would mean that there is no solid you.

The you is always changing, depending on the other objects that are within its perception. The you is always in comparison because all the objects are continuously in movement, which would mean that comparison is also continuously changing. It can begin to be seen that there is no fixed you, only descriptions happening with the body. Those descriptions aren't really accurate because they are mere descriptions that are in a language. There is most certainly **not** a somebody, or fixed "you," **in** there.

What happens with this me/you energy is that it attempts to stabilize itself, and attempts to keep in place all the movement and appearances, in order to be fixed and solid. It tries to make a solid "someone" out of itself, in order to maintain its being as a separate entity. It's like it is always clutching and trying to grab air, because that "who" that you think you are is always in movement and never an actual reality. There is a continuous struggle to make yourself a something and make the others a something.

A description is something that was used in order for humans to progress and evolve. Who you are cannot be a description of the body. A description of the body arises in *this*, in what you are, which is every-thing and no-thing.

There is something that has always been here, that never moves, that is still, with seeming movement happening in it, that is no-thing, and yet every-thing.

It is loud and it is silent.

We can call it *Aliveness* but it's not really *Aliveness*. "Aliveness" is just a very narrow and tiny word that we place upon it to try and talk about it. The comparison of Aliveness would be deadness, so you can see how rubbish the word "Aliveness" can be.

This is something that cannot die, that is always here. It's absolutely free, this Aliveness. It's boundless and not caged in any way. Within it, dreams of being caged appear. It dreams in an entity that seems to be separate from everything and is bound in description and comparison.

One side of this Aliveness is not happening; it's empty and still, so still that it is beyond the word stillness. The other side is all of these forms appearing, many different forms, that are made of the same thing. These forms are all seemingly moving and transforming from one form to another form. There is no form in which "you" are, yet there can be a character appearing and disappearing, a character which is a description of the body-mind mechanism.

This is not who you are or who the other is. It's an appearance happening that comes and goes, just an appearance, and not a truth. It's always moving, and there are no fixed characters. Characters are always changing and growing and developing. There is no free will in the choice of the characters. There is just movement and an appearance of choice happening that is coming from this no-place, this nothing-ness. ~

Worth

The thinker is drawn into the drama of opposites called good/bad, right/wrong, should and should not. The way that this separate energy functions is through a sense of not feeling good enough. When anything in the flow of life triggers that, it will then go into story-land to try and avoid that feeling. 'They should not have done that, they are a bad person for saying this to me.' These stories happen to avoid that full-on sense of unworthiness. It all comes down to unworthiness, not good enough, or that feeling of being rejected.

The way that separation happens is through a sense of lack. That sense of separation goes into stories and tries to cover it up. Normally the "me" goes into a particular story saying, 'I'm really bad for doing this.'

(Guilt.) 'It's their fault and they should not have done that.' (Blame.)

There is so much happening during the day that can easily trigger that sense of "not feeling good enough." This sense of lack and separation spends much time seeking to get out of "not feeling good enough," rather than feeling the burning sensation of it. If it were just the burning sensation of "not feeling good enough," surely it would just collapse in on itself.

The stories show up and then there is a seeking for pleasure to avoid the pain, because if it gets to the pleasure, then it thinks it will feel good enough, and this will make it all okay.

It is a funky drama, and it sure creates a lot of them, especially with the relationships or the money. These are the big dramas. The triggers that give that sense of not good enough are different to each body-mind mechanism, or each "me," because of the conditioning and genetics.

It may feel like the centre of you is in the head, or the neck, or the chest, or groin, like you are a somebody in there, a "me." It may **feel** like you are the thinker, creator and mover of that body, but actually there is nobody in there. There is nobody in there creating thoughts or action or making the heart beat. There is nobody in there making the eyes look, or the ears hear, or producing urges, or decisions, or intuitions. It's all coming from no~where, or emptiness, or no~thing. This no~thing is every~thing that ever happened and every~thing that will happen, which is also no~thing. ~

Body

What you think you are is not true. If you think that you are a good person, a bad person, a right person or wrong person, all of that is not true. There might be a description of the body, in that a body might have done something bad or good, but it is not a truth in any way.

Language is in comparisons, so there can only be comparisons, so it cannot actually be true. What we have taken ourselves to be is the description of the body, whereas the description of the body is just something that is used in order to communicate. Doing something bad, or forgetting something, or even being a peaceful person is not an actual reality. Even if you were a peaceful person, in comparison to the Dalai Lama you might find out that you are not. No language can be true, yet we spend most of our time living in this mental reality, this **idea** of ourselves.

This mistake of believing that you are a somebody inside the body, and a description of the body, has become an energetic experience. It really **feels** like you are inside a body and controlling the body, and making the body's reality real, and that you are somebody separately walking through life in time. You **think** that you are the past actions and future actions, things that you have done and things you are going to do.

It **feels** like thinking and action is coming from inside the body, but really the body is empty – *absolutely* empty.

This emptiness is continually being covered up by a dream of being a someone in time. This idea makes *this,* or what is actually happening, to be seen through a lens or a veil. It is not "you" as a separate entity; it's you as a separate entity interpreting what is happening with all your past and future experiences. What *is*, is then not seen as it is, but rather it is seen through a film or veil of "you."

You are not the body and you are not the story, but rather the body and its story are arising *in* this. Reading this may begin to loosen that focus on "me, me, me" in time, and that energetic contraction of a "me" in a storyland. In a way, nothing will loosen anything or not loosen anything, because it is never really even happening. ~

TAO TE CHING, Verse 40

The Way is a circle
It always returns, it never ends.

A bird flies through the air
Leaves not a trace
Tao gives birth to everything
Takes it all back into itself
As if nothing ever happened.

From: Meditations on the TAO by Stream Ohrstrom

One-ness

Anything that is ever spoken about non-duality isn't *it*. Any speaker that you admire, any teacher that you look up to, anyone who is speaking about non-duality, isn't speaking about non-duality. They are speaking or using language that is duality.

You can never speak about non-duality because nothing means anything. Every word that was ever invented is a sound, which humans put meaning on in order to communicate, and they think that they are actually communicating about something.

All of this is meaningless, and none of it has any meaning at all. The word "computer" does not really mean a box that is humming. Lisa writing and me reading, it doesn't mean anything. It's all just an interpretation in order for us to communicate. It isn't wrong or right.

What has happened for the human being is that communication, or words, have become more important, or more real, than what is actually happening. Words are always in opposites and always in two-ness, where there is always a comparison. To know light there has to be dark; to know me there has to be you. Words will always give an appearance of two-ness or duality.

This is not a dualistic world. This is *One* energy expressing itself in creativity.

When the conceptual reality begins to crumble, along with the one that is claiming the conceptual reality, then what *is,* is left. *This*, which is not two. No-thing. You can never see One-ness, yet it *is* it.

If you could see One-ness, there would have to be an outside of it. There is no outside or inside, it's *all* It.

Isn't that so exciting. ~

Separation

The individual personal energy is convinced that it is acting, or making decisions and choices, and having at least a bit of influence in the flow of things. It believes that it is deciding to move the hand, or to put the kettle on, scratch the ass, or stroke the dog.

Maybe it doesn't believe that it has *all* control, but it does think that it is influencing things in some way.

That is not the case at all, not true.

That personal energy of "me," and the storyteller of it, is simply a by-product of what is happening. They are not creating anything, or in control of anything. They are just a part of the flow.

The designed program is to give the appearance that somebody is separate, and somebody is in control of his or her life, and living separately from everything else. That is not the case at all, not true. ~

Overlooked

This is the easiest subject possible, but because it is so easy, it is overlooked all the time. The "me," the person, is looking at thoughts and ideas and trying to find ways to describe what is happening in time.

Because the focus is on that, it misses what is actually happening, which is freedom right here, the stillness that is right here. The person is always looking at what the thoughts are saying 'Freedom is when the body stops being angry, or when the body is blissful.' or when this happens or that happens.

Those are thoughts, and it seems to the person that it is an **actuality**. And it seems impossible to understand that they are just thoughts that come and go *in* something.

The freedom is what they are appearing and disappearing *in*, not what they are actually saying or thinking. It's so simple, but really complicated, for that one that is looking for things, or looking for understanding or knowledge, or even a way to describe it. But it's not really about that.

It's about *This*, which is indescribable.

The thoughts will look at me being silent and think that then it's about "me" being silent, or they will see Lisa being in movement and think it's about the movement. You may even think it's about looking into my eyes, but all these are only thoughts that come and go. These thoughts are not speaking truth at all.

When you try to describe the taste of watermelon, can you actually describe it? Nope.

The person is always trying to put meaning on everything, and nothing has meaning. It's all meaningless. All of this appears without meaning. Meaning appears *in* it and disappears *in* it.

The thought right now might come up, 'Yes, this *is* it.' **That** is just a thought.

Peace

Love is what *Is*. I cannot see love as ours or yours, that would be love with conditions. Conditioned love is about trying to get something, or trying to give that love **to** someone. Love is what *Is*. Love is the essence of everything. It's not that helping a dog or rescuing a dog from Thailand doesn't happen. I just rescued a dog from Thailand. It's not that those things don't happen, but it's not "my" love. It wasn't that "I" decided to **do** that. Life wrote in that momentum.

Because life is in opposites, there is always going to be decay and destruction. It's a part of what happens in this. There is never going to be a peaceful world in what happens because the way in which life is set up is for one form to change into another form, continuously.

At the same time, it's happening, and it's not happening. You could say that there is a side where it's not really changing or moving, and a side where movement is happening, and in that movement it's always one form is changing into another form. As soon as one form becomes its most beautiful, it then begins to decay and be destroyed and change into another form.

There is never going to be peace **in** the flow of life. There is never going to be this peaceful idea that people long for. That peace is an illusion. It's all about mental concepts of how we would like it to look. It is what it is, and *love* is the end of the resistance **to** what it is.

That doesn't mean that helping and bringing the dog back to England doesn't happen, but it's not mine. I'm not compassionate. I'm not claiming any of it. That to me is the arrogance, is the mistake. It's just something that happens, in *love*. It also works the other way around. Take the murderer or the paedophile: if that's the character that is played out, then that also doesn't belong **to** them. This role doesn't belong to someone. It is just what's happening.

I see love as being completely impersonal. When love is personalized, then it's 'What can I get from that person? How can I give them my love or how can I get love from another?' When it's not personal, then love is everything, and everything is constantly changing into different forms. There is always destruction happening as well as growth, but it's not personal. When it's personalized, then the suffering begins. ~

Fading Game

The way that life sets up separation is by dreaming in a separate entity in the bodies. It dreams it in by a combination of thoughts, feelings and an energetic contraction that makes it feel like there is a centre inside the body.

What it does in order to create drama, excitement, agony and despair, is that it writes in the separate self, which is a sense of not feeling good enough. This sense of self lives in imagination-land and it is consumed with thoughts of having to find its completion and wholeness in the future, in the things, or in the objects. This separate entity starts with an energetic contraction that makes it feel like there is somebody inside the body. This apparent "I" has an agenda, and that is to find an object to make it feel complete. The contraction starts, and it's off to find what it is looking for in the future.

Life creates amazing games.

Non-duality has a way of making it sound bad, but it does create some amazing excitement. Dogs, birds, insects do not have this. It's a whole different form of experiencing, this apparent separate identity that identifies with objects. This separate entity has the feeling that it is separate from everything else, and it is on a special mission to find its own completion. It creates a load of tension in a grand drama of 'When am I going to get there? Is it in this?' It creates great highs and great lows. People will work twenty hours a day looking for this. They buy huge cars and huge houses looking for this.

There can come a time when this looking becomes exhausting and the interest in the game fades. At this point, it has become uncomfortable, and non-duality begins to be entertained, or they go on medication. They may even go to classes to learn to hope again, trying to find the hope in an object that will satisfy.

There is nothing wrong with this game of hide-and-seek, but it can get to a point where a lot of things may have been achieved, and there arises a sense of discontentment with it all, or a sense that you will never find it, followed by exhaustion. It begins to become apparent that no thing will ever fill that hole or make you feel good enough.

Actually, all of these findings in themselves were designed to do just that, to never satisfy. The "game" was to constantly look, because you were never designed to find what you were looking for.

What may happen in this non-duality is the collapse of that game, and then there is just what *is* left. Without that game, there is a huge part of experiencing that will be gone, and the "me" doesn't want itself to go. It wants to find the thing that will complete it. I assure you, it never will, because no-thing **can** complete it.

The "me" looks at that collapse as a huge thing that it will get, but I assure you, it's never going to get anything. There will simply be the collapse of that identity, which is the end of the game.

What will be left is just this, just what is happening. There will no longer be a person that is trying to get somewhere, or analysing how it feels, or work out how it feels.

Ecstatic

I don't know if I even talk about non-duality, actually. I don't know what I really talk about. There's great joy in expressing that.

There seemed to be a person here who was suffering and didn't like life, that didn't like who she was, and always felt uncomfortable. There was something hurting in the torso. That person seemed to question what she thought she knew about life and what she thought she knew about her suffering. The more and more that happened, the less and less she seemed to know about life and what was happening.

There seemed to be a point where it stopped happening for her anymore, and that person that suffered disappeared. All that was left was love for what is, which had been there before, but the focus was always on the person, and what the person knew about themselves, and the world.

Then there was this body that carried on acting in this world, carried on with its beautiful and strange conditioning, but it was no longer for anybody anymore. It was no longer "me in relationship with what I knew." There wasn't this constant me, my life, what this means, where is it going, what should I do, where should I go?

It was just *this*. And this is ecstatic to *be*. Ecstatic, because it *is*.

If freedom is truly wanted, which is not an individual thing, then the heart of the individual person has to be ripped out. Because everything you think you know about life has to be questioned. Everything that you've been taught about importance, and right and wrong, begins to crumble.

I found that I lost knowing who I was anymore. That sounds really weird. I just lost myself. There was something that had always been there still there, but it no longer belonged to somebody, it was happening. There was this energetic change where I was looking at the world inside the body, and it was almost like I was watching myself in the brain, experiencing life. It was like I was more up here, (in my head), than in what was happening, the dream was more important; of what I was imagining others to think of me, what I wanted to portray myself to be, it was just up here (in my head), and then that energy just stopped and it just went back into what was happening.

There's a really beautiful quote from a film called *Her*. Now, I'm just going to make this quote up to suit myself, but it's similar to the real one. There is this couple, she's a computer, and he's a human, and this computer has been given the ability to evolve. Because she is an operating system of the computer, and she can evolve, she goes through this whole drama of falling in love and all these different things in the film. She begins to experience wanting, wanting lots of things. She has a lover that is human and she begins to explore that, and then she begins to suffer, really suffer. She then begins to fall in love with lots of other humans, and she begins to have lots and lots of lovers. This is her conversation with her original lover after she's been through this massive journey. He says to her, the computer, 'Why are you leaving me?' because she says she has to leave now. And she says, 'The reason I'm leaving you is because it's like, I've been reading the story of our love, and I love the story of our love so much, that I've begun to read it really, really slowly. And the slower and slower I read it, the bigger and bigger the gaps become between each word, until they've become infinite space, and this is where I reside now.'

She disappeared into her story. It's like you disappear into this. Before, I was telling the story of me, of Lisa, Lisa, Lisa constantly. Stories of what she's done, where she's been, where she's going, what she's doing, who likes her, who doesn't like her, what the problem is, why psychologically I'm suffering, and when am I going to be enlightened. It was so here (in the head) all the time. Then, more and more, the story of who I was got questioned, and something happened where it cleared. Who you truly are dissolves back into everything. You fall out of yourself.

It's no longer that you're hiding behind the head and the stories any more, or that you're in relationship with the world. You ARE the world, you *are* everything. It's no longer "you" having to deal with the world, and "you" in relationship with "other," it's a dissolving back in and you completely disappear. This is happening for nobody, it's happening in absolute stillness, because without that story, who is this happening to?

It's just perfectly still, it's absolutely empty. That stillness is so incredibly beautiful. It's who you've always been; it's just been focused on that person going back-forwards, back-forwards, back-forwards (in the head). It's everything. Everything is what you've always been. You've always been everything.

The longing for love is really a longing for home, but we believe that home is in the flow. And this is why non-duality has nothing to teach; it's just trying to constantly point to what it's not. Mind can spend hours in trying to convince another that it's right. It can spend lifetimes trying to put a certain number in the bank. It can spend a lifetime trying to get love from a husband, and it will always fail, because the only love is what is, and that's absolute love because everything's always been embraced and appearing in what is.

The story of loneliness is a really beautiful pointer, because the separate self is trying to look for company in love from others, it's trying to look for it in the next moment with a partner or with the kids, or with the right housing situation. And the end of loneliness is that everything is surrounded by that love, because it's appearing.

Dog

I have a beautiful dog, and I love watching her. She has no idea that she's alive, and she has no idea that she's going to die. She has no idea if we're in a dangerous situation, or if the situation is good. She has no idea about any of it, and the response in the body-mind mechanism is absolute happiness. The side effect in the body, because she has no idea who she is, is joy. Spontaneous joy.

Whatever happens, she's totally in it. She's totally involved in it, and that total involvement is absolute love. She's in love with anything that's appearing, no matter what it is; she is 100% in it.

There's no sense that it's happening to her or that she gets 10 years of life, 14 if she's lucky. There is no sense that she's got to have a happy life and make the most of it, or that she's got to be rich, successful, slim, and have lots of babies.

She just is. In every moment she simply is. For nothing, she has no reason, nothing. She has no reason to live. She doesn't even know she's living. She's just living.

But, this is a but; she's not a perfect body-mind mechanism. Now I know this is really hard to believe, that a supremely enlightened person doesn't have a friendly dog, but it can happen. She's a vicious dog, she likes to bite, well, she doesn't bite, she's never bitten, but she likes to go, rrrr, rrr, rrrr, if people she doesn't know stroke her. She also likes to fight with girl dogs, and she never, ever, ever wants to share her food. Ever. She likes to roll in poo. She does the dunk and dip. We call it the dunk and dip because she's walking along, there's a bit of poo on the floor, and she just dunks her neck in the poo. She particularly likes if it's from swans or ducks. Duck perfume.

She never suffers. Ever. Even when the cat chases her down the street and she's crying, even when she's scared or shaking, or if I'm telling her off, or if she's growling at somebody, there is never, ever an ounce of suffering, because it's not happening to somebody, it's just happening. There's no energetic contraction inside the body that feels like life is happening to her, and that she needs her life to be a certain way.

She just is. Just is. This is all I talk about, just a pointing back to what's actually happening. You will never, ever find what you want in what you think you know about yourself and life. You will never find it in life changing, or life being a certain way. You won't find what you're looking for in anything you know, including anything that I've told you. The only place you'll find what you're looking for is this. This is it.

This is not intellectual. This is not something you know; yet it is. It's what's always been here even though forms seem to be changing. It is always this. This is home, this is what you look for, but it's got nothing to do with you and the body. The body appears in it. It's not coming from the body.

You just need to look at your dogs. Any animal, really.

It's a great thing in a way, spirituality, because we learn all these things that we think we need to be, like a kind person, or a better person, or a healthy person. We think that something is good, in that it challenges old ideas of what we were. But then we get stuck on these new ideas; that healthy eating is it, or that anything in the world is it. In the beginning, the challenge of ideas can be very freeing, but we often then stick on the new ideas. It's really not about being anything in the manifest world.

It's not being a good person or a healthy person, but if there's somebody who's been in prison for 20 years and is convinced that they were right in killing someone, talking to them about compassion may destroy those old ideas. They'll most probably become a pain in the butt preaching for compassion. They might now believe they've got something and they're higher than others because now they've learned you've got to think about others. This new belief might feel more liberating for them than the world of hate they used to live in, but it's still another position, and it still is in relationship with badness.

The idea of being a good person and helping or being nice to others is still an idea that belongs to somebody. It might be more liberating than another position but it's incredibly arrogant for somebody to think they know what goodness is. In a way you could call it hate. How would you know what goodness is?

In the changing of ideas, there always comes great freedom because you lose old ideas, but taking on new ideas is to go back into that suffering game. In the moment of giving up old ideas there is great freedom because it was always ideas that were the problem. Always. But then to go into goodness ideas, or rightness ideas, or what you know to be right is just to zip yourself up into another straight jacket.

So the idea of this is to become like a dog. That's it. We'll all be like 'woof, woof.'

The human will always have intelligent thinking, but what does seem to be being removed more and more in humanity is the idea that who you are is the body and that you are an independent person moving the body in a separate world. Thinking is a natural function like the heart beating, it just happens, it's a functioning, and intelligent thinking can still occur. The separate person was never doing the intelligence. The knowledge to drive the car; to type or to think was never done by the separate person. I don't even know what you call it; it's chemical reactions happening in the brain, it doesn't belong to anyone.

What does seem to be being switched off more and more now, is the illusion that the intelligence and that life belongs to someone, that there's somebody experiencing life, and somebody separate from life, and most importantly (which is in the human dynamic), is that there's somebody victim to life. Most body-mind mechanisms have that dynamic that says "I'm victim to this."

It might even be playing out in this book now. It may feel that you're being victimized by my speaking, and that very feeling, if it is arising, is the very core of the sense of self. The way that the thinking functions, the person functions, is it moves away from the feeling, so then it becomes "her" fault, "she" is creating my unhappiness, because she's not giving me what I want, in whatever way, maybe you're thinking "She's speaking incorrectly.", "She's putting it in a bad way." or "I should be up there not her." Whatever it is, the person jumps straight away into the fault of my unhappiness is because of what's happening to me.

There is no world out there happening **to** someone. There is just *life*. There is just life. And you *are* life, but not you as a "who you think you are."

The following is a compilation of questions and answers during talks with Lisa in various cities or villages all around the globe, as well as live streaming online. The names of the questioners have been left out and in no way represent any person that can be named.

Love Affair

Q: *When and where is the thin line between our own effort and life itself?*

Lisa: That is such a sweet question and that is where the juice is. There is no line; it's all one movement. Life itself and the body's actions are the same thing. This means that there is no one acting, no one choosing, no one separate from everything else. It's all one big movement. The really crazy part of it is that as that energy of the personal begins to crumble, it's seen that movement also has another side, of absolute emptiness or nothingness as well.

Q: *I know that everything is life and that you and I are life, but is there any chance that something happening* *somewhere in the world is not only life itself but also something happening because of someone's mind?*

Lisa: No. Nothing is separate. That would imply separation.

Q: *When you are enlightened, you love every single part of the manifestation of life, and you just experience this experience in the body and these conditions? Can a murderer be enlightened?*

Lisa: This is not you experiencing life or you loving everything. As the "me" dissolves, you will see that everything has always been love; everything is an act of love. Everything is love manifesting nothing. All of this is an absolute love affair.

The character doesn't love everything, the character likes and dislikes that is its job, but you aren't the character.

Can a murderer be enlightened? There is no murderer. There is no separate person. All of this is dependent on everything else. It's all one thing. The murderer and the saint are the same movements. The abused and the abuser are the same movement.

Q: *Does he kill because of the experience in the body and these conditions in his mind, and his own way of thinking?*

Lisa: It's because that is what Nothing-ness created. That is what Love created. It's full-on, this subject. It happens the same way that the saint happens, the same way as the thoughts appear, the same way as the light, the trees, the sounds, the smells. It's all coming from no-thing, appearing and disappearing back into no-thing. Seemingly in the story, you might find patterns of the mind in which the body could be described but that isn't relevant to what we are talking about. ~

Positive Thinking

Q: *Is there ever any point to try and think positively and optimistically, or will life just do whatever it does? Does this mean that whatever happens is just perfect?*

Lisa: The assumption in the first part of the question is that you are somebody separate that has control over thinking. That "you" is a thought that has seemingly become an energetic contraction or an expression in the body. So there is a thought, 'I am going to think positively,' and then a positive thought comes up and is followed by lots of feelings and energies that give an appearance of a "you" choosing.

The question isn't 'Should I think positively?', the question that I ask is 'Who is this "you"?'

Could it be that the "you" is just simply a description of what is happening, rather than the source of the action? Is the one that is saying 'I am doing, I am choosing' really the chooser, or an illusion that gives the appearance of a someone?

I am pointing out just the thoughts here, but it's the energy that they come with which is the true deceiver, the energy that you are found in the body and you are thinking these thoughts. Who? Who can think positively? ~

Home

Q: *I've been watching teachers for two years now, since discovering the sense of me being no-thing about two years ago. Now I am only waiting. And I want to go on more, but I am so tired. I am writing this in tears, and I just want to come home. I have no idea how to get home. My mind rushes when I try to be alone. I don't want to rush or not rush, and I don't care of this foolishness either. I don't want to meditate and only remove the fact that I am not here for only ten minutes. I don't want to rush the meditation either, but my mind is telling me to stay here until I am free. I feel I will be here looking under every rock for eternity, and I am so tired of waiting. I don't want to hold on for a few more years. I don't want anyone to tell me to wait, and that includes my bad habits and the lack of my focus. A year ago I could see clearly that what I am writing to you now is bullshit. I wish I could explain what I am trying to say. I* *just want to come home, and I don't want any more things or any more questions of 'Who am I?' without dissolution of the seeker. Even if the seeker is present, what to do, even in this?*

Lisa: This is just one big fat lie. The one that is saying it wants to come home doesn't want to come home. It wants to stay in drama and it wants to play in games. It's just a lie. It's just a veil. It's not even a lie. That is too dramatic. There is nobody telling a lie. It's just a veil coming up giving the appearance of a somebody who is frustrated and fed up with the spiritual path.

That very voice that is saying all of this is the "I", **is** the seeker, is the veil. It doesn't want to come home, it wants to seek. It appears that the game is set up to say that it wants to come home. The mind or ego is set up to seek for home, but it's also designed to never get home because the getting there means the death of the seeker, of the "I". The seeker is the one that lives in time and space and stories.

Right now what you are saying to me is the whole boo-hoo drama of 'I want to get home, but I can't find my way home.' It is only a veil, a thought, and that thought comes with an energy that contracts and feels like suffering. That, too, is an illusion.

More than likely, what is happening there is that hope is being stripped away, and now the mind is playing despair because it cannot hope to be something, or to be enlightened, because there is nobody that gets enlightened. This is the death of the "me."

Right now it is playing the despair game instead of the other game of 'I'm going to get there, I've seen those things, I've seen it and I've understood this, and I've listened to all the books.' Now it's playing, 'I can't get there.' They are both the same trick, they are only opposite ends of the "me." You did not see nothing-ness. Who is the one that saw nothing-ness? Who is the one that is claiming that it saw nothingness?

That is **all** an illusion. The ego is most probably having such a tantrum that it will go along the sense of 'I want to throw myself off a bridge or under a car.' Tomorrow it will be like, 'Yes, I'm so enlightened because I've got this and I've done this or I know this.' Those are all stories in space and time, and this is the end of stories in space and time. This is the end of the one that can say they are enlightened because there is no "I," there is nobody.

Just *this*, just life happening.

Just *Is*. ~

Quite

Q: *What happened for you?*

Lisa: I don't *really* know. I can tell you a brief flow of the events, but after it first happened, (this might have been identity coming back, I don't know), the mind was like, 'What the hell? What did that? What did that?' At first, it kept trying to formulate that immediate prior into some system, like, 'Why? What?' The flow of events seemed to fit into what other speakers have spoken about, and seemed to fit into the typical pattern of a lot of things very quickly getting taken away, a lot of things that I thought I couldn't live without, or feared that I couldn't live without.

Prior to that, I'd been through the typical middle-class conditioning of the west; university, dysfunctional family, trying to make a career. I started seeing many different talkers on non-duality, and studied Buddhism for 5 years.

After many years of all this kind of investigation and looking, life physically took away the things. I'd heard continuously for years, 'It's not in the things, it's not in the objects, what you look for is not in the objects.' I knew the subject inside out, back to front; I used to listen to it going to sleep. I spent months going to see Ramesh Balsekar speak every day.

I knew it very well, I was still convinced, though, that liberation was going to be intellectual, that I was going to understand something, but it was actually the reverse. I lost all the things and ended up in Asia with very little. No friends or family. I felt incredibly alone. I also realized it was exactly the same as when I had all the things, it wasn't any different. In the moment-to-moment eating, brushing your teeth, talking, it was actually exactly the same, just with different scenery.

There was this incredible aloneness, very human loneliness. There I was with nobody who could physically support me. If I got hit by a bus, no one would know I died. And then I began to look at the room and it started to vibrate, which is really silly, but it did.

I kind of realized, without it being intellectual, that I'd never been alone. I actually needed none of the things that I thought I needed, and I'd never truly been alone. I looked at everything. I wasn't abandoned by my lover or my friends, or my family, I hadn't lost anything. I was still in *it*, if you know what I mean. I'm so sorry that my words are so messy sometimes. I was still in it. It was still *this*.

A few other little things happened. (This was just an experience, and most probably not what's going to happen in other body-mind mechanism experiences.) Everything began to shake and vibrate, it was like….to go to the toilet at night, I had to walk along this corridor with a low wall, and if I didn't walk straight I would fall of 2 stories. It was like everything was vibrating and I had to walk straight. That was how I could tell how much everything was moving.

Those experiences were just a weird side effect that happened in the brain, it happened for maybe a day or two, and then one morning I went to a café. I had very little money left, and I was like 'Fuck it.' I ordered banana fritters and ice cream for breakfast, and a pot of tea. I was listening to trance music, and I was just soooo happy, eating my banana fritters. They tasted so good. I didn't care about getting fat, or the fact that if I ate it all, I'd have to have another nap after so much food, or that I'd lost all these things, or what I was going to do now. I was just sooo happy with the banana fritters.

Then, I looked at the waitress and I was like, 'Wow, she is really beautiful.' And then I looked around the room, and I was like, 'Wow, I've never noticed what a beautiful café this is.'

Then, this energy changed. I couldn't know it, I wasn't inside my body anymore. I couldn't register it any more because that thought functioning wasn't happening. For two hours, I walked around and I was just overwhelmed by the beauty, but I couldn't know the beauty. I had no sense of registering it. I could only know it like the *aliveness*, in the instant moment of it. I could only know it in that instant, so I couldn't know that anything had changed.

The big thing in my story was to "Save the Animals." I was one of the protesters. There was a dying dog on the street, covered in fleas, skinny, and in a terrible state. Before I would've looked at that dog and seen this poor, abandoned animal that nobody loved, but I saw that the dog was absolutely bathed in love. It was not a separate dog being abandoned, that was always imagination.

Nobody dies alone, they don't even die, it was just love happening.

That was shocking, but again, I still couldn't register the shock. That was the experience. That was an experience that a lot of people report, but what happened in that, was **not** the experience, that wasn't the important part.

The important part was that Lisa had stopped experiencing the world, it was completely empty and all that was left was *love*.

Love is involvement and intimacy with things. The discomfort always came through the reflection of self and what I thought I knew. When I saw the dog before, I saw Lisa as somebody who'd been chucked out and abandoned by life, so when I saw the dog, dying by itself, all I saw was Lisa's abandonment. I never saw something. When that stopped, all that was left was love, because that's the nature of everything.

Not love as a feeling. Love as an intimacy, emptiness or a fuseing experience.

That was quite an answer.

Samskaras

Q: *Recently I went to a meditation and there was a feeling of a cleansing of the Samskaras.*

Lisa: Samskaras being the habits or conditioning?

Q: *Yes. At this time there is a sense of choosing and also a sense of not choosing. There is a feeling of me being here and the wheelbarrow is over there. I seem to be going between those two states, where there is no sense of choosing and then there seems to be a sense of choosing. There is space, and then there is no space. It feels like it is coming and going, this choosing. At times it's like all the things that I have ever heard in non-duality completely make sense, and at other times it feels like I am back to being separate.*

Lisa: It can feel very frustrating, this stage. It can be incredibly frustrating to be not having any problems and being absolutely free just doing whatever appears, and then that one comes back in and questions it all. It can feel like the character's becoming a bit schizophrenic in a way, because it is flipping from this tight energy that takes things personally, and then in the next moment there is this freedom and everything is okay. It is very confusing because you can feel like a really unreliable character.

Q: *(Laughter) Yes, and it feels like there is this sense of absolute ease, and life is a piece of cake. There is no choosing and it's just life unfolding, and it's just what is in front of me, and it's so easy and so simple. The words of this are absolutely not important.*

Lisa: The teaching of non-duality is no longer a problem.

Q: *Yes, and then something will contract because maybe there will be anger coming at me, or I seem to get hooked into something and I can feel the contraction. There is something in me that is still remembering that the illusion of "me" needs to play out. There is a part of me that knows that it is just the "me" playing out.*

Lisa: It's an energy that is unwinding itself. It can't be any other way when it is there. It's not like you did something wrong for it to come back in any way, or you are missing something. In most cases, it seems like there is a deconstruction through time. It slowly chips away at that energy and that energy runs itself out. Eventually though, what will happen is that the idea that you have deconstructed through time will begin to deconstruct, and it will be just an idea that there was a process. It can seem like that person is slowly unwinding and the energy is just running out. It's much like fire, the wood burning out. For a certain amount of time, that energy can keep fooling itself that freedom is in the future, or in the other person being a certain way. Eventually, it loses that energy.

Q: *Yeah it just feels like something is playing out. It does feel very different ever since the weekend with you. There really are times when there is no "me" energy and even when the "me" energy is there it is not taken seriously.*

Lisa: Before, the suffering used to be so serious and the energy would come up and say 'Why is this happening to me? It's always like this.' But it's not always like this. It is just that in that moment the energy has put all the stoppers out. All of that is such nonsense and it slowly burns out. You might have said those words one hundred times and then finally something sinks in, and you will say 'What a load of rubbish.' In a moment this will change.

Q: *You talked about how everything is just changing all the time, and something heard that anyway.*

Lisa: The process will begin to make less and less sense. You won't even be able to wrap that up anymore. You won't be able to comprehend the idea that you have lost something. Then it's just what's happening. It's just eating dinner, such simple living. There is such freedom in simple living. Living without the abstract idea that "you" are living or that you're a good person, right person, happy person. It's just life that is happening. ~

Self-Inquiry

Q: *Do you think the method of Self-Inquiry is useful?*

Lisa: Nothing is useful. It is always *This*. If self-inquiry happens, that's what happens. What it leads to is absolutely irrelevant. **This** is where the juice is; this is what's happening. It's not in where you're going to get to tomorrow. That's carrying on in the dream of "me."

The "me" is always in time. If self-inquiry happens, it's not right or wrong. The idea that you are going to get somewhere is a total daydream. Where are you going to get to? It's always here. When is it not here, *this*?

What is happening is that you are imagining the body, or yourself, which isn't even you, in the future, being better. That's exactly like being better with the money and imagining the money. It's just like imagining the big boobs and being better with the big boobies or a big dick or a beautiful face.

Self-inquiry is no different. It's exactly the same mechanism of the "me" dynamic.

Where is there to go?

This is what's happening and it's always what is going to be happening. The love affair is *this*, not tomorrow's daydream. We will never know tomorrow and we will never know yesterday. *This* is what IS. ~

Thought

Q: *How do you manage thoughts when they show up?*

Lisa: Thoughts are just something that appear, another part of appearance. The assumption is that those thoughts belong to you and that you are controlling them or producing them.

How? How do you produce a thought? It can only be a thought that could think it could control or change a thought in some way. How can you change a thought when they appear from an absolute mystery? They come into appearance just like everything else but there is another thought that assumes that "you" think.

The "me" dynamic is so funny. It's claiming everything. 'I think, therefore, I am.' I Am, and *in* I Am, thinking arises. This assumption of control, that is what creates the suffering. It's an energy actually of 'I am the controller, I am the doer.' The thoughts say "I" control and "I" am choosing to pick thoughts or look at thoughts. You think your discomfort is because of **your** thoughts? It's not. Thoughts appear and disappear. The thoughts are normally talking about past and future. ~

How Did This Happen?

Q: *So if there is no "you," how did I get this "you?"*

Lisa: I will give you my explanation, but ultimately all words really fail. If we take a look at the animals, we can see what it is like to have no sense of self. Animals do not perceive that they are a body or emotions or thoughts. They don't have self-awareness. What animals experience is just Alive-ness and what is happening. To them there is no inside and outside world. Because they don't have a sense of self, they do not suffer.

What happened with humans is that they began to have complicated thinking, and they began to see in apparent time. Animals have a sense of time, but they don't really perceive it. Humans began to describe the actions of the body in time. Animals have more of an instinctive perception of time.

As this complicated thinking grew for the human, this entity in time became stronger and stronger. Where I'm going and what I've done only happens in time. As this complicated thinking seemed to grow for humans, what also began to grow was this apparent separate entity that lives in past and future projections. Rather than the time being something that appeared when it was needed for normal functioning, it became a veil or filter, and suddenly life or living was not seen as it was anymore. Instead it was seen through this filter of time, and life became about "you" **in** time, relating to life.

Before the complicated language, there was no "you." There was just *life*, not you in a story of life. What you are is that original Alive-ness, that Being-ness that is prior to the story of you. It was there at birth before the whole story of you began. That's the freedom that I am pointing to that has always been here. That Alive-ness that is prior to 'I am the body' has always been there. The "me" person thinks they are the story, and all suffering happens in story time. All of the anxiety, the worry, the blame, the guilt, the shame and the pride, that's what happens in time. In this moment, in this Alive-ness, there is no suffering. *The suffering is only in a mental and conceptual reality.*

The animals experience pain, but there is nobody in there holding on to that pain. The pain just comes and goes and the pleasure comes and goes, and they are not seeking for a better state because they don't have a sense of self.

The you is a conceptual sense of self. You are not the body. You are not your past or future actions. There is this Alive-ness that's there always. Its free, still, and moving at the same time. There's an element to it that is silence. It's emptiness. You may have heard of this empty silence in Buddhism or other traditions.

Q: *So we are betrayed by symbols?*

Lisa: No, not you. You're not betrayed; "you" are the betrayal. "You" is the lie, because **who** are you? Which one thing can you say you are? The only thing that is is Alive-ness, and we can't find Alive-ness. It's every-where and no-where.

Q: *Consciousness creates the capacity to see in symbols or to symbolize, no?*

Lisa: It creates the ability to dream, yes. It creates dreaming. By consciousness I assume that you mean what I call Alive-ness.

Q: *To symbolize, in the moment in which there is this capacity, what happens is that the reality is exchanged with* *the symbol and we start believing, or consciousness starts believing, in symbols and sounds, and just loses the reality and lives in this?*

Lisa: It doesn't actually lose it; it's never even touched. It really is like when you put the film on; you are never lost in the film as such. There is the film playing and that's all there is, the film playing. We describe ourselves as lost in it, but you're never really lost in it. Consciousness never really gets lost in anything. It's just producing this dream that's very strong and exciting. Consciousness cannot be lost. Alive-ness cannot be lost in it. Alive-ness **is** what is producing it. When it produces it, it feels really real, but for nobody.

Q: *The aliveness is the only real thing then?*

Lisa: It's a funny word, this "real." The constant is Alive-ness. The constant is a Being-ness. There has to be Being-ness, and all forms are moving in Being-ness. I don't really know what real or unreal or truth or not truth is.

Q: *What is time in this?*

Lisa: Time is something that arises, which is a functioning. When time is needed in order for functioning to happen, it arises and then it's gone. Time is subjective to the one that perceives it. Time is different for a child, an old person, a mentally disabled person.

It's subjective. It's moving and it comes and goes. The question is what does time appear and disappear *in*?

This. No-thingness, which is timeless.

Beautiful. ~

Daily Living

Q: *How do you function daily if there is nothing to attain? Is reaction more of a flow or dance as opposed to a need or want that you have to do?*

Lisa: The body just does it. It is set up to get food and shelter, the material things. It just happens to take care of itself.

Q: *Do you find the more you let go, the more the body flows to the next event?*

Lisa: That's what seems to happen here, but I don't know about others where the apparent "me" has fallen away. They may have easier or more difficult lives. Here, life is very easy. But some people may think my life is terrible because I don't have a house. Money comes.

There is not a "you" going out and getting things. It's just happening.

Q: *What about planning. You don't really plan?*

Lisa: Yes, things get planned but there has never been a "me" doing it. We're so convinced that there is this action and we are in control of it. Right now the hand is moving but no one is moving it. That is how the whole of it is working.

It's where the money is being obtained and how the driving is being done and how the relationships are working. It's all JUST happening. We have spent what seems like agony over the getting of the money, but the "me" was never doing it. The body did it. Life is now easy, but I'm sure a lot of westerners may think, 'How terrible. She doesn't have a pension or a home or any security.'

Q: *So then you're saying you are not making any choices?*

Lisa: Choices are always happening, but there is not a somebody who is doing that. Choice appears from space. When I was a kid, I'd be walking and say, 'Look, the legs are walking.' I would be so amazed by that.

It has become so uncomfortable because there is a fighting with what is happening. The struggle is for the one that thinks it's doing life because there has been such a strong imagining that you are in control. The imagining of giving up that control for "me" is terrifying. You are not rich because of you, and you're not poor because of you. It's simply what life has done. No one has ever done anything, ever!

The psychopath is not separate at all from the saint.

Q: *So then, everyone is innocent?*

Lisa: Yes, but that is saying that there is something to compare innocence to, it is just what *Is*.

Q: *So I'm not the bad character, but I'm also not the good character?*

Lisa: Right. Most of us like to think that we are the good character.

Q: *So there are no great artists or musicians. They are just what is happening?*

Lisa: Yes. If you think about singing, how do you make that sound? How are we making any sound?

Breathing in, breathing out,
Moving forward, moving back,
Living, dying, coming, going –
Like two arrows meeting in flight,
In the midst of nothingness
Is the road that goes directly
To my true home.

Gesshu Soko

Falling in Love

Q: *I had a realization that I got into the Advaita and liberation thing because I disliked this character so much. I really wanted to get rid of it because I hated it. After hearing from you last Wednesday, I realized that bad is as much loved as the good. I could really feel the truth of this, because for the first time in my life I felt so relieved. I am now starting to love this character, and treating it with love and respect instead of trying to kill it and get to some imagined liberated state that I have in my mind. Thank you so much. Your words have done me good.*

Lisa: Yeah, most people are trying to avoid themselves until they realize that this is about falling in absolute love with yourself, to the point of falling so much in love with yourself that you disappear into that which is loved.

The one that is falling in love disappears **in** that love. Most of the time people say things like, 'This is bad. I have to get rid of the ego.' This is about an absolute falling in love with that person, as it *is*.

There is a quote from a film called *Her* where she says, at the point of leaving her lover, in the explanation, *'It's like I'm writing a book, and it's a book I deeply love, but I'm writing it slowly now, so the words are really far apart, and the spaces between the words are almost infinite. I can still feel you and the words of our story, but it's in this endless space between the words that I'm finding myself now. It's a place that's not of the physical world. It's where everything else is that I didn't even know existed. I love you so much, but this is where I am now, and this is who I am now, and I need you to let me go. As much as I want to, I can't live in your book anymore.'*

Beautiful. ~

You mistake sweetness for Truth.

You are drawn to the gentle smile
The reassuring gaze.
The soft voice
And kind word.

If it makes you feel good enough
You assume the hand of God
Has touched your heart.

It is the cruelest trap of all
And you keep falling into it
Lured by the promise
Of goodness
Of progress
Of attainment.

You pass the Sage
So crude and ordinary
Without a glance
His common words
Mere animal grunts
In your ears.
Ram Tzu knows this:
The path to Salvation
Is in the dirt you step on.

by Ram Tzu

Rape

Q: *I got abused verbally and was also abused sexually by my father. It is very hard for me to meet him, but sometimes not avoidable. I am busy with thinking on how to fix this pain in me. I've tried a lot of techniques and healing treatments but the pain comes back again and again. I often think I have to fix it by talking to him and making him aware of the pain he created in me. It does not feel like it would work to make him stop or help me to heal. He often speaks in a very aggressive way to me, or puts me down. I get frozen when he does this, and inside I feel so much pain. The suffering gets even worse after, when I try to find words in my mind to stop him from doing this. All that happens is silence and becoming frozen when he does that, and then there is a feeling of pain inside. Do you think you could take that? How would you deal with it?*

Lisa: I am the worst one to ask this sort of thing to. The last time this subject was brought up, I got quite a few angry e-mails.

You suffer not because of what your Dad does, you suffer because of you. To put it better, there is suffering because the "you" energy claims it.

You can't fix life. Life is a series of pleasures and pains, and it does its little dance and it's completely unfair. Some things life does are so cruel, and some things are beautiful. That will never be got out of, this cruelness, or the beauty. But that's not the problem, believe it or not. The problem is the one that claims it, the one that believes your father sexually abused you and that he **chose** to do that.

Q: *So I am the abuser and the abused?*

Lisa: Not "you" as the story or the character, but as Alive-ness. The character is the one that is abused; one character abuses another character. All of it is Alive-ness.

The suffering comes with that energy that is taking it personally and wants to get out of the pain and wants to get away from that sense of 'He abused me.'

The body naturally moves away from painful situations. The body will naturally move away from somebody that beats it unless there is "me" energy there that says, 'I should take this beating. I am guilty, I deserve it.' It would just naturally move away.

If someone is holding up a stick to the body, the body would normally move away. If the father body were continuously hurting the daughter body, the daughter body would naturally move away from that. But it's not you deciding to do it. Often that does not happen, when the personal identity is claiming it. Believe it or not, there is more than likely energy in that story which is feeding off of it. The me is feeding off of that story, it's addicted to that story, being the abused and the victim, being the frozen one.

It's very uncomfortable and very painful, and there is loads of suffering in it, but it's alive. That person is alive and has a drama, and has something to get away from. That energy is something to sort out, and it gives it someone to blame, somewhere to go.

Q: *Well, the story is that I want to change it and have a loving father.*

Lisa: The father is how the father is. Freedom is not in what you think the future should be. Freedom is here. Right here there is no abusive father and there is no abused. There is no father that doesn't love you or father that does love you. Right here, there is just freedom.

The flow of things cannot be any different. In the flow of things, if the dad is beating the daughter, that's what's happening. The "me" energy is saying, 'I want a loving father and I'm going to stay here until you love me.' It's impossible. It is as it is, that character is as it is.

The perfect life is not about having two parents that love you. Happiness is not having the flow of life being a certain way. The flow of life is as it is. The freedom is the end of the one that takes it personally. The freedom is here, this Alive-ness, this silence and this stillness.

Q: *So would you not try to talk to the so-called father body?*

Lisa: Whatever happens, happens. Look at how you are trying to plan it, living in this conceptual reality. **That's** the suffering. You can't plan life. It is, as it is. This is the freedom.

Q: *More than likely it will happen again and I would like to have something I can do.*

Lisa: Yeah, so then you will think about something you can do, and more than likely that body will do something. Freedom is not about you doing something; it's not about "you". What you are looking for is *this*, the intimacy of *this*, not dreaming about changing the world or changing the father or changing yourself. 'If I stand up to him,' that is not going to give you what you want.

Q: *Can there be freedom in abuse while it is happening?*

Lisa: Yes! Yes, otherwise it wouldn't be freedom. I'm sorry. Why does this young woman have to be the one that is saying all of this?

It would not be freedom if it were only found in peaceful situations. What I am talking about is absolute freedom, not freedom that is only found in non-abusive perfect situations.

Q: *No, thank you. It's wonderful you say it. And I somehow know it, but it is good to hear.*

Lisa: So few people will say this to you. Most people will sit there and say, 'That's terrible.' They will support your story that you are a victim and that you have had a terrible life, and that you have got to work it out with your dad and forgive your dad and make him realize that he has done something wrong.

The statistics are that one in three women are sexually abused as a child. You ask 'Can you have freedom from abuse?' Yes, because that means if this wasn't the case, then women cannot be free. *A third of women are sexually abused.* That is not saying that the body won't move away from the body that is forcing itself on it, but that is not what is being talked about here.

What is being talked about here is freedom in any situation, whatever is happening. It's not about you fixing the future. The freedom is right here in this Being-ness that is boundless. It's in absolute torture, the murderer, in war zones, the paedophile, in everything there is this freedom. There is freedom for the abuser as well. Nothing is excluded from God.

Freedom is not found in releasing this emotion or imagining yourself in the future and behaving differently. This is what therapy will say, and it is just supporting the story. The freedom is now, in listening to the bird singing, the light, the computer, the hum, the taste of the tea.

Q: *Thanks.*

Lisa: It's you. ~

Source

Q: *What is the source of this energetic expression of "personal?" And why is it so powerful if it is illusory? And why does it have a specific location of here versus there?*

Lisa: The Source of everything is never going to be known; all there is is Source. All there is is God experiencing itself through the apparent separation of objects.

What is the Source of everything? Every-thing and No-thing. Not one thing, and everything. You can't ever stand outside of everything and look to see what it is. There is just Source, and it is not one particular thing.

The energetic contraction is part of this expression. It is not separate from this expression. Separation does not really exist, it only appears that way. It is very strange and impossible to talk about.

Separation feels very real because that is what it is designed to do. It's designed to give the appearance of a "somebody" that is separate from life. It does not really exist, this separate person. What is, is *this,* the sounds, smells, sights, feelings, etc. *In* that, the first abstraction, which in a way isn't even an abstraction, is "I" am experiencing *this,* rather than just pure experiencing, without an "I." The abstraction arises *in* experiencing.

It is not wrong and it does not need to be denied. It is just a description of what seems to be happening. It isn't who you are. In order to experience, there needs to be an object to be experienced. All there is, is experiencing, and it is so intimate that there is no separation between the experiencing and the objects; they are one and the same thing.

All these questions, they all come down to not knowing. Right here, right now there is just one big *not-knowing.* There is a knowing of experience, but nothing to be known in thought. There is just experiencing. Everything in thought is hypothetical; this would mean that there is knowing, but also not-knowing.

We never know the answer to who we are, or why this is happening, or how we get rid of the energetic contraction. All of that is La-La Land, it's hypothetical.

The only thing that is ever known is experiencing, which is pure, simple and immediate.

Description of what is happening is just a description of what arises in Alive-ness by an apparent character. The apparent character is only one form of expression. There are billions of forms of expression in *this*, and all of it is what *is*.

None of it is ever personal. ~

Forms are limited by their shape;
Nothingness is infinite,
all – pervading,
and ceaselessly interpenetrating.

Andre Doshim Halaw

Purpose

Q: *I get the impression that to the mind it's more fun to seek and think I'm getting somewhere?*

Lisa: Yes, completely. But in that world of dreaming and getting somewhere there is always going to be the not-getting there as well. It's going to come with both of the stories, the highs and the lows, the 'got it' and 'lost it' because the world is always in movement. You get the lover, then they're gone. You get the best car and it eventually rots. This is a huge loss, a complete loss of that part of experiencing and dreaming that you are going to finally get there. All of this dreaming of getting these things and then losing them, it's all temporary. This is about losing your best friend **and** your worst enemy.

Q: *So am I right that the "me" loses its purpose when it stops seeking?*

Lisa: Yes, and it really hates that.

Q: *Well, then there is really nothing to do anymore.*

Lisa: There is nowhere to go because there is not even a "you" there that is going anywhere. There are just forms appearing and disappearing.

It's so undramatic in a way, and yet dramatic because the forms are always moving. It's terrible because there is nowhere to go if there is no imagination. There is nowhere to go and there is no future.

This is suspended in nothing~ness. Absolute meaninglessness.

What love. ~

All You

Q: *There recently was this woman who sat and let me vent for like twenty minutes. She didn't say anything to me, but she just looked at me with her eyes and there was just this love that let me feel what I was feeling. I remember the first time I saw your YouTube video, your eyes reminded me of hers. When she looked at me it was like all of a sudden my heart just melted with her love.*

Lisa: It wasn't "her" love, because there is nothing external to you. In that moment, the "you" collapsed and that love was experienced, and then you said, 'It's in her eyes.'

It was your love, always, even when you looked into my eyes.

Q: *Was it because she looked into mine?*

Lisa: No, no, there is no her. What happened in that moment was "you" collapsed and then there was love. You interpreted it as her love in her eyes. It's always been you. It couldn't be anyone else's love. It couldn't be you as a character or something limited. It's you as that Alive-ness or Being-ness. There is nothing outside of that. It's just that you think that you saw it in a form, but it's always been you.

Q: *It's most beautiful, right?*

Lisa: Yes, so beautiful. Everything you've ever fallen in love with is you.

Q: *We spend so many years trying to find the perfect boyfriend or perfect this or that, and it's always been here?*

Lisa: All of those forms just come and go, and come and go. All of them. You can never find it in a form because it is their nature to come and go. There is no form. That's why they are always moving.

Q: *That's really beautiful.*

Lisa: It is really beautiful, though it can sound nihilistic at times. It's a total love affair when that person that is always making sense of things begins to drop. It is like that drawing board you had as a child. You create on it and then it is erased forever.

Q: *Sometimes, with my cat, I sense that absolute connectedness. With humans it seems when I have this sense of separateness, I have to set boundaries.*

Lisa: It is never you doing it. It happens by itself. It's got nothing to do with "you." You don't have to assert boundaries. "You" don't even have to look after yourself. The urges and the impulses are already happening in the body before you make up the story to it.

Science is now proving that the brain has the activity of saying something six seconds before you even claim that it is you doing it, before it comes out.

Q: *So the body just at that moment knows what to do?*

Lisa: Yes, always. It knows what to do. The question is, 'Who is the one writing the impulses into the body?' That's the most amazing part. The storyteller always comes after. They can scan the body now and see that activity is already happening to make a choice before you consciously think about making that choice. It's amazing that the thought is appearing after the action.

We are so convinced that that is who we are and that we are choosing, whereas the claiming is just a side product that has happened, like an over-excited activity of the brain or an energy that is claiming things. You never need to make boundaries, boundaries will happen. When you're sitting there thinking, 'Should I tell him no or should I tell him yes?' it's already been decided. It's already happening in the body. The answer is already coming.

The personal activity is absolutely useless.

Q: *Thank you.*

Lisa: Thank you.

*Had I not known
that I was dead
already
I would have mourned
my loss of life.*

Ota Dokan 1432-1486

Loss Program

Q: *I have noticed a few things lately, for example; the assumption we make that there is such a thing as past or future outside of thought. It struck me that life or being can only ever be present. It doesn't ever have a memory, and who is there to own a memory? Who does a memory refer to? Also, with the fact that everyone and everything appears within awareness, so the idea that when we leave to go to work, there is a house or a family back there continuing to exist independently can't actually be true. How could there be a back there? It's all what is appearing now, only this. Life is so much simpler than thought makes it seem.*

Lisa: For sure, and for the dogs and the animals and the young children or babies, that is all there is. There is just what's happening, and they are not constantly being this other reality reconstructed with a past or future, what

I'm going to do, what I haven't done, I'm a bad person or a good person, or I don't have a big enough house, whatever it is. It's just what's happening, and in life there is no suffering.

In *this*, this doesn't suffer. It's only in time that suffering happens. And even the "in time" happens here, it's not actually happening in time. There is only an appearance happening of time, of past and future, 'I've done something wrong, I'm guilty.' And it comes with this energy, 'I'm a bad person, I don't like them, they shouldn't do this.' It's all in time.

For the dog, if there is anger or another dog annoying it, it just growls and its got no sense that it should or shouldn't do that, or that the dog is going to have hurt feelings or whatever it is. There is just what's happening in the moment. The human does have the ability to comprehend past and future, and that's not a problem.

What has happened in the human is who they are has become past and future, or become a person in the past and a person that is going towards the future. So there is nothing wrong with the fact that humans can comprehend this dance of past and future, but it's not who you are. The past and future always arise here. It's not that this is because of the past and future. That is the assumption of the mind and a very simplistic way of thinking. Humans think they are so intelligent, but this way of thinking is very, very simplistic.

Sometimes, I think the more clever the people are, the more stupid they are, and the simpler people are the less stupid people. Intelligence is way overrated, way overrated in our society. It's hilarious because in non-duality, intelligence is also put high. It's put high in society, so that intelligence is king. It's put high in non-duality, but it's got fuck-all to do with intelligence.

It's that intelligent thinking that has created a false world, a false you and a false I.

Tree 1: What did you do to lose your leaves?
Tree 2: Nothing, it just happened.
Tree 1: But what can I do lose my leaves?
Tree 2: Nothing, it will happen when it happens.

Student: What did you do to lose your 'I'?
Teacher: Nothing, it just happened.
Student: But what can I do to lose my 'I'?
Teacher: Nothing, it will happen when it happens.

Paul Smit

What Can I Do?

Q: *I know you say there is nothing to do, but I still need to ask this question. Is there anything I can do? Like the 'Who am I?' practice? I mean, is what you say any different from the 'Who am I?' practice? Is that what you really say? There is nothing I can do?*

Lisa: Have you heard me say that? There may be, I don't know. What I am questioning is the validity of that "one" that says 'Let's go and get something better than this for the future.' It may sound like I am saying there is nothing you can do, but I don't ever directly say that. What I tend to do is question the "you" that thinks it is the doer of life and its actions and where it thinks it is off to.

If the 'Who am I?' question arises, then that's what arises. The assumption that 'It's going to go somewhere and get something in the future to complete itself.' is the lie. The future is just an assumption. What is is *this*.

Q: *Well, I was thinking that whichever happens is right. Whether I find a teacher that tells me to ask the question 'Who am I?', or someone that questions the "me," they both push me to absolute frustration. The quicker I am pushed to that place of frustration the better.*

Lisa: That's so cute, but all of what you just said is making sense of it again. Ultimately, this is all a mystery. The only thing that is, is *this*. What is. What you said is a theory arising **in** *this* but it's not known to be true, it never can be. It always remains theory; words put together that appear to make sense.

What seemingly comes out of Lisa, a lot of the time, is a questioning of who this "you" is, and what this "you" thinks it knows. Whether this leads to frustration, someone walking out, bliss, laughter, or the collapse of the "you" is not known. ~

The Guru's Lament

*They think they are broken,
Aching and finished, despairing.
They sit with me and their energy fills the room,
Sweet liquid blackness,
Tortured and strong.*

*Their tragedies spoken,
Quaking voice, just barely daring;
Their imagined shortcomings revealed to me,
Secrets to witness,
Kept overlong.*

*(Keep us safe 'til we are whole
Gently guide us to our goal)*

*How dearly they struggle.
They conjure my silence
Into just what they need:
Father or saviour, hero or scapegoat,
The faithful mirror, the love
On which they feed.*

They never know it at first,
But they are perfect; there is never anything wrong.
Just as they are, they are perfect;
Perhaps they'll realize they were perfect
All along.

(No, no, no, no, no, no more
Will we wage this fruitless war)

When I first started, I thought I could help them.
Believed that their suffering was wrong;
At last I can hear them,
Beautiful song.

Desperate pleading,
Always convinced I can cure them,
Undivined divinity reviled,
They are exquisite,
Violent or mild.

(How we suffer, oh so needy
For sweet comfort we are greedy)

There is no medicine.
Nothing can save them, they are saved;
We sit padmasana, invite revelation,
Celebrating regret - the endless mistakes they have braved.

We may never realise we are perfect,
There is never anything wrong.
Just as we are, we are perfect.
Perhaps we'll realize we were perfect all along.

(We will heal, we will see
What we need is to be)

- Suzanne Foxton 2013

Doer-ship

Q: *It feels like I am doing something wrong?*

Lisa: You can never get life wrong. Life doesn't belong to a somebody in time. It's happening, and there is this energy, this extra part that life plays, an energy of claiming life, 'I am choosing, I am doing.'

Q: *Through you Lisa, words often arise like 'It can be written in the story that my boyfriend will support me or cut me off with money. It's all God's will, it is just what is written.' Can you expand on this?*

Lisa: When I first started talking about this, there were still quite a lot of sentences and language that came from Ramesh Balsekar or Advaita, words like 'God's Will.' Often, Ramana Maharshi or Ramesh would use the term 'God's Will.' I stopped using it because it starts to get really confusing. What I mean, is that 'God's Will,' or nothing-ness or life is *that*. *That* is just what's happening.

Q: *Yes, because I have read in quite a few books that 'It's just what's written. Action happens because it's written.' The resonance here is that there is a bit of a destiny.*

Lisa: In Indian Advaita and non-duality they do use a lot of those words, and it means very different things to them. It isn't the way that we interpret it in the west. It's not that there is destiny or that it is written, because there is no one writing it. What it is trying to imply is that the one that thinks it is doing life isn't the one creating life. It's going to happen, in that the story is always going to be the way the story is.

The story is spontaneously appearing **now**; it's not that it's already been written. In another way you could say, like Ramesh used to say, 'It's in the can.' The film is in the can. The way it was interpreted here, 'in the can,' is that it is all arising now, or it's all done.

Everything in the "you" story is arising now. It's not that it has ever happened. All the ideas of "you" are happening **now**. It's never the future. All the ideas of the past are arising now. It's all appearing spontaneously here.

Ramesh used to use the word destiny, but destiny to him wasn't so much about the future. It was more a questioning this idea that you are the creator of the story, that "you" are the doer of your actions. He spoke very differently from the way that non-duality tends to be in the west, particularly with words like "God."

I love the word God, but I don't use it so much anymore because in the west it is so confusing. He used to call this all God.

What Ramesh is particularly pointing to is non-doership, the one that thinks that it is controlling and writing its life, and writing its future and creating for the future. Not very many teachers confront this. Most teachers are still talking as if somebody has control.

Here, this seems the most important point in non-duality, because if somebody is controlling life, then that means that there is separation, or two-ness. A lot of teachers do not confront this subject.

It's very popular now in non-duality to say that you **do** have control, and you *don't* have control. I would not agree with that at all. The way that it is seen here is that there is an appearance of choice, but there is nobody choosing. There might be a thought that says, 'I'm going to choose apple juice over orange juice,' but there is nobody choosing at all.

Q: *I am very much thankful for the clarity.*

Lisa: Happy to chat with you, thank you. ~

La-La Land

Q: Have you read *A Course in Miracles,* and what do you think about it?

Lisa: I haven't read *A Course in Miracles.* I know bits and bobs about it. I think there is some nice stuff in there, but I think it really encourages the intellect, which isn't necessarily a good or a bad thing, more than likely the mind will focus on intellectual understanding, and it's not *in* understanding this. It gives a lot of concepts for the mind to comprehend and think that it has understood something and got something and gotten somewhere.

This is an absolute loss program. It's really not about intellectual understanding. That's just what the mind thinks.

It's the loss of all of those ideas of who and what you think you are, until there is only an absolute mystery. It's not even about the idea that you're aware, or consciousness, or knowingness, even those are ideas. It's just mystery.

There is just what *is*. There is not even someone that knows they observe, or something observing, because that is still knowing something, that is still a division. It's the collapse of every idea.

A Course in Miracles has a lot of ideas. I think it says it very simply, they sum it all up in like two sentences in the beginning of the book, and then it goes on to write a very thick book about it. It gives exercises, and the mind thinks, 'Okay, so I'll do these exercises and we will get somewhere, and this is going to help me and I'm going to get somewhere.'

It's all concepts. It's all living in La-La Land, in a reality of somebody separate from the world making its way back to non-separation. It's craziness. But there seems to be some nice stuff in there as well, some quotes that I've heard that seem sweet. It's so easy this stuff. The mind always wants to jump on the bandwagon of 'What can I do?'

This is a loss program; anything positive that the mind takes on **isn't** *it*. It thinks, 'Oh, okay, everything is an illusion, and that's the way this is.' The mind thinks that

that's a truth. I know that *A Course in Miracles* talks a lot about this being an illusion, but that's absolute bollocks. That's a concept, a positive concept. It's not *it*.

It's not about living in positive concepts. If you take on anything Lisa says in a positive way, as if what Lisa says is the way it is, then again you have positive concepts about *this*, which isn't it. This is a loss; there is no middle way. This is an absolute loss of everything the "me" is always trying to get.

Q: *Okay, it's true mystery is nice. When I get what you say, I can feel my body, and I feel good. Why do you think that is?*

Lisa: I get the sense that, as whenever any concept is lost, there is always a sense of relief, because concepts are binding. They give this appearance of being contracted and tight. It's just that an idea falls away and there is a relaxing that happens. The natural way of life is no suffering and pure Being-ness. Pure Being-ness does not suffer.

Being-ness dreams in this apparent suffering, which isn't really happening. There is this suffering of 'I am somebody and I know things.' and this contracted energy begins. As these ideas fall away, that contraction seemingly dissolves, but it's never really happening at the same time, which is kind of crazy.

Q: *Life is awesome, thank you.*

Lisa: It is. When there is so much focus on the thinking, and who I am and what I'm doing, and where I'm going and what I've got to choose, then it can seem very agitated or uncomfortable. But as that dissolves, I mean, this is *miraculous*, there is always so much seemingly happening, and spectacularly it is not happening at the same time.

When the "me" has got ideas of what it should look like, and what I want my life to be, and how I want to be seen, then it becomes very narrow, which is another expression as well.

Here, there seems to be an exposing of that. ~

Reality

Q: *I feel quite fed up and exhausted in listening to spiritual teachers telling me what reality is. It has been a pastime for a long time. I listen in moments and find some agreement or peace or something. Is there really anything to lose by listening to them, as part of me still assumes that there is something to get? It seems that the answer is that whatever happens will happen, that I have no choice.*

Lisa: The answer actually is nothing. It's even more than whatever will happen will happen, or that you have no choice. It's nothing. The other side of nothing is everything.

Forget all those teachers telling you all of those things, and I'm one of them.

It has nothing to do with the teachers or the words that they say. Life is just playing the game of Lisa talking about it. The answer to everything is no-thing, and no-thing's partner is every-thing.

Every-thing and no-thing. Maybe you could say what is, is *this*.

The mind is like 'Yeah, but....'~

"It's like you took a bottle of ink and you threw it at a wall. Smash! And all that ink spread. And in the middle, it's dense, isn't it? And as it gets out on the edge, the little droplets get finer and finer and make more complicated patterns, see? So in the same way, there was a big bang at the beginning of things and it spread. And you and I, sitting here in this room, as complicated human beings, are way, way out on the fringe of that bang. We are the complicated little patterns on the end of it. Very interesting. But so we define ourselves as being only that. If you think that you are only inside your skin, you define yourself as one very complicated little curlique, way out on the edge of that explosion. Way out in space, and way out in time. Billions of years ago, you were a big bang, but now you're a complicated human being. And then we cut ourselves off, and don't feel that we're still the big bang. But you are. Depends how you define yourself. You are actually – if this is the way things started, if there was a big bang in the beginning – you're not something that's a result of the big bang. You're not something that is a sort of puppet on the end of the process. You are still the process. You are the big bang, the original force of the universe,

coming on as whoever you are. When I meet you, I see not just what you define yourself as – Mr so-and- so, Ms so-and-so, Mrs so-and-so – I see every one of you as the primordial energy of the universe coming on at me in this particular way. I know I'm that, too. But we've learned to define ourselves as separate from it."

– Alan Wilson Watts

Conditioning

Q: *Conditioning is happening, yes?*

Lisa: Yes, the body is always conditioned. When the baby appears, the body of the mother is conditioned to act motherly. I am not speaking about the way the body acts. Whatever the role that it is playing, it does its role. The role that we play is constantly changing. In every situation and with all of the people around you, it is constantly changing. There is no basic, *one* role.

Q: *What about emotions. Are they still happening for you?*

Lisa: Yes, but they don't belong to anyone anymore. It was always the idea that they belonged to someone which was the suffering. It's not 'I am sad.' there is just sadness or happiness, and it is free to be what it is. It does not belong to a someone. There is not a "should" or a "shouldn't" happening anymore.

Q: *Does the conditioning get less?*

Lisa: The conditioning of the body?

Q: *The thoughts and habits.*

Lisa: The body is always going to be conditioned. The conditioning may become easier, but not necessarily. What I am talking about is the absence of personalizing the conditioned body. In spirituality, often the focus is on improving the conditioning, which isn't wrong. If the conditioning is improved, it may be a better experience. But that is all that happens, there is just conditioning being replaced with new conditioning. I am not speaking about the conditioning of the body.

I am speaking about the one that is personalizing the conditioning. The body is always going to be reacting in some way, or conditioned in some way.

Q: *This change of conditioning that you are talking about, is there a concept of progress in the conditioning?*

Lisa: No. It doesn't matter. The one that cares about the way that the body is acting is gone. So the body can act like an idiot or a saint, but there is no longer someone in there saying, 'You shouldn't be like this.' It's certainly not about becoming a perfect body-mind mechanism.

Q: *This Oneness is here, but still there is an element of evil and there is an element of good in this world, in this manifestation?*

Lisa: Yes, and there will always be both. There will always be peace and war.

Q: *Couldn't the world progress towards more peace?*

Lisa: The only reason that you want peace is because you are afraid of war. The body is going to be destroyed; everything is going to be destroyed. And in that destruction there is birth and it starts again.

Q: *There is no individual soul and there are no choices?*

Lisa: No. ~

Irrelevant

Q: *You speak a lot about an energetic contraction from the "me". I don't really see what you mean by that and the liberation of the energetic contraction. Can you say a bit more about that?*

Lisa: Do you feel bound to the body, inside of the body?

Q: *Sometimes, yes.*

Lisa: That's what I'm talking about.

Q: *Most of the time I have the feeling that I am inside the body.*

Lisa: That is what I am talking about. That can collapse, and then life won't be taken personally when that collapses. The body is just another object arising in no-thingness, in oneness. It's not anymore a "you," it's another object appearing and disappearing. It's very simple.

Q: *For me it is something very conceptual, because I have no feeling of this energetic contraction most of the time.*

Lisa: Yeah, a lot of the time it's not there. The base feeling of the energetic contraction is 'I'm not good enough, I have been rejected.' It's an energetic feeling of 'This isn't enough.' I suspect that it is there a lot of the time, but it's just not noticed because a lot of the time the focus is on the flow of things and what is happening. I suspect that quite often there is that niggling sense of 'This isn't enough.' Some of the time it might disappear completely, but nobody is there to know that. No one can report about it or tell stories about it because there is no one there. You would not know it; you only know when you're there.

Q: *How do you know that it is completely gone?*

Lisa: You don't know because you don't exist anymore. Do you know when you're driving the car, or hang-gliding or taking off in an airplane? There is just pure experience happening. The person that is seeking, loses interest completely, so it's not an issue at all as to whether it's there or not. That's just completely irrelevant.

Q: *I notice it when there are thoughts about the future or past, the feeling of an individual living in time.*

Lisa: Because that's the only thing you can notice about who you think you are. It's not who you are. It's just a description, a description of the body that has become who you are, which isn't who you are. It's another thing that comes and goes.

Q: *The problem for the seeker is that it becomes another goal?*

Lisa: When that energy is there, it will latch onto anything it hears and sees. It will be your boyfriend's or girlfriend's fault, or it will be the fault of the teacher, that you haven't got liberation. It will be the fault of work or because the coffee is not good enough. When that base sense of "not enough" is there, then everything will be blamed and latched onto as a potential better future. That is just the way it is when that energy is there.

It's a double-edged dagger, talking about this, because in some ways there can be a hearing of this and a knowing, beyond the words, what's being talked about. There's a resonance that *this* is what is looked for, this is it. It's really beautiful that this can be heard.

The word *this* can also be heard, and there can be another mission of **getting** this – in other words, another thing for the seeker. It's a sad tragedy because in one way this message is expressed, and in another it will just become another way for the seeker to repress what it is feeling and try to get to something better.

That's the way it goes. If I thought my job was to liberate people, or use these words to help people, I would be very troubled. It would be a terrible job.

Q: *Sometimes there is a resonance with what you are saying, and an acceptance with what is happening. Most of the time I am completely lost in thoughts and trying to get out of the thoughts.*

Lisa: The base thing that it is trying to get out of and trying to avoid is this sense of not feeling good enough, or that it has been abandoned in some way. The base sense of all seeking is 'I am not good enough to be loved.'

The "me" is desperately trying to run away from that feeling. It blames people and feels guilty to try and get out of that feeling. That **can** collapse. When there is just that feeling of not good enough, everything collapses. It is kind of crazy though, because when it's there, there is a looking for a way to get out of it.

It can't be got out of. If there is pain or discomfort, then that is what is happening, and **that** is *it*. There is an illusion there, that there is somebody there that can potentially get out of *it*. That person is not the controller of life, it's just another thing or creation appearing **in** life.

Q: *A lot of teachers speak of this collapse of energetic contraction, and that becomes something to look for. Some teachers don't speak about this end of energetic contraction. It appears to be a very attractive thing. For you, would you say that it is a complete end of thoughts?*

Lisa: It's not the end of thoughts. The appearance of choice will still appear, but it is the end of suffering.

Q: *I wonder about the complete collapsing. Is it really forever?*

Lisa: I didn't say it was forever, you said that. I don't think about forever.

Q: *Because you know that things are changing all the time and nothing stays the same, what is this "me" exactly, because I cannot find it? I look for it through self-inquiry and I can't find it, so what is this "me?"*

Lisa: The "me" is this energy that feels like life isn't enough, but it's not really happening. And it feels like it exists as somebody in time, and that people do things to you and you do things to other people, and that you have choice and free will and things to obtain, and a life to live for the future.

Q: *Well that is known to be completely false, in a way.*

Lisa: It can be known, but it can still be appearing, until that energy falls away which is impersonal. If I wanted to be more scientific about it, I could say until some chemicals change in the brain, or the brain switches over to stop creating the false sense of I, then suffering will appear.

It's so unfair that there is not a pill that you can take. It's really unfair that it just drops in some body-mind mechanisms. For some, there is no way or particular path, it just happens. I really hear what you are saying. I may really screw it up when I speak about it, but speaking about it happens. It has to be spoken about in some way.

How can I speak about it without making it sound like it *is* something? Even if I just spoke about awareness, and did awareness teachings, it would still be a big deal. If I call it *'The Awareness,'* it would still be something for the mind to get. It would then try to sit in awareness. There is no way to speak about this without the "me" hearing it and seeing it as another carrot to get to.

I can hear your frustration, and it's sad that there is not a button that can be pressed to stop it from coming and appearing.

Q: *It's strange because I cannot tell you what I am looking for.*

Lisa: What you are looking for is that strong sense that says 'I want to be loved.' to go away.

Q: *I don't know what it is.*

Lisa: You just want that sense of not feeling good enough to stop arising. That's all that's wanted.

Q: *In comparison with other moments where there is no sense of something being wrong, etc., I can't compare the state of peace, or not thinking, or rest. I don't know what this liberation exactly is about. It's completely mad.*

Lisa: Yeah, that's for sure.

Q: *I know that I have a preference for peace, but I also know that that is just another state or experience. It's nothing because it comes and goes.*

Lisa: What I am talking about is the end of that one that is trying to hold onto those states. It's not perfect pleasure or perfect happiness; it's the end of that one that is trying to hold onto something.

Q: *How do you know exactly if this "one" will not reappear?*

Lisa: I don't, but I don't give a fuck. (Laughter between them.)

Q: *How do you have a certainty of that?*

Lisa: I don't. I don't have any certainties, but I am also not sitting here worrying about it coming back. There is no interest in those thoughts. There is no interest in fearing the future.

Q: *You wouldn't be able to tell if that sense was definitely gone?*

Lisa: No, you're looking at things in a really warped way. You think the way that you are looking at things is logical and makes sense, but you're looking at things through words. 'How do you know it's gone?' 'How do you know it won't come back?' None of this makes sense. You think it does because you have meaning on every word. This is IT.

Q: *But you know, when the contraction....*

Lisa: No, I don't know all these things. All I know is a comparison, which is really fading, to a before. It's reminded when other people are speaking to me and it is just an image of that energy that used to appear, of feeling not good enough and not worthy.

It's absolute bollocks, liberation. There is no liberation. **You** can never know it. You can only ever know the comparison to the before.

I also meet lots of other body-mind organisms that are constantly talking about their suffering, and I am reminded of how humans think. To you the idea of it coming back is a really logical question, but to me it is really strange. You are listening to me and thinking that there is a person inside this body speaking, but that's all your projection and imagination. When that drops, there is no imagining happening. There's just no-thing, not even no-thing, because that is still a word.

Q: *But there is a body-mind talking.*

Lisa: There is a body talking, it seems there is, but ultimately that's really not happening. What most body-minds think is happening is that there is a separate entity inside that body-mind organism choosing to speak like this. It's sad that this not feeling good enough happens for the human, but it is still a very convenient evolution for the human. It works really hard because it's trying to feel good about itself and trying to avoid feeling not good enough.

Q: *When there is very big pain in the body, something very uncomfortable...*

Lisa: That's just pain. It's not a problem unless somebody claims it to be mine If there is not somebody there, then it's just – (Interrupted by questioner.)

Q: *So you're saying you don't have thoughts of wanting to fix it? They don't appear?*

Lisa: If the leg has been cut off and there is really intense physical pain, then the body will seek to relieve the pain. But that doesn't mean that there is a separate entity inside the body. Pain only becomes agony, which is suffering, when there is that "me" there that feels like it's happened to you, and that you're not good enough. That's the real agony of life, that energetic contraction that feels that sense of not good enough.

Q: *This energetic contraction is very strong when there is pain in the body. If there is no pain, then all is okay and there are no worries.*

Lisa: What do you mean by pain? Because that energetic contraction is very painful in itself.

Q: *It is the physical pain that brings on the energetic contraction.*

Lisa: It is very painful, the energetic sense of not feeling good enough.

Q: *For me, there is no way out.*

Lisa: No, there is no way out, and that's the tragedy of the human. It's always believing that it can get out of something. The animals don't daydream about it. If they are dying or in agony, their leg has been burnt, they are not sitting there dreaming about something else. There is just agony.

It's crazy, because we consider hope as a beautiful thing in the human functioning, but it is what creates the separation and the lack of love. The word that you are going to most likely hate is love, if you hate energetic contraction.

All of this is an absolute love affair, which includes the pain sensations. Everything is touching, and it is so intimate, it's beyond intimacy. That sense of 'This isn't good enough.' or 'This shouldn't be happening to me.' blocks the love, although it's not really blocking the love because that is happening *in* love as well. It sort of covers it. This is the tragedy for the human.

When agony and pain and discomfort are happening, that's what happening. There is no way out and it will be there until it stops. Most people don't want to hear that. They want to hear the message of how can I use what Lisa is saying to try to cover up the agony of feeling rejected and feeling not loved?

It can become agony. It is agony especially when it's triggered in the flow of things like the lover going off with someone else, or the money is all gone and there are no friends. All of these trigger that same sense of not being good enough.

Q: *Reading books and staying on the path seems to have helped the contractions.*

Lisa: Yes, but there has never been any you that is doing it. If the "me" is to be deconstructed, then it is happening like everything else, on its own. The person wants to constantly look at itself and say 'How do I get there, and where shall I go?' That's all a lie.

You are never going to get yourself enlightened. The "you" dies, but **you** cannot kill *yourself*. It will keep on wanting to tell the stories of how it is getting closer, but it only wants to tell them to feel better because of that sense of not feeling loved. When it tells its story about being nearer to liberation, it feels a bit more relaxed and less abandoned or less not good enough.

Q: *Most of the teachings now teach that you can approach this thing by self-inquiry, meditation or direct looking, and it's very misleading for the seekers. They really think they can do something.*

Lisa: Yes, and that whole time, they are dreaming that they are doing something. That's just them dreaming they are doing something. Doing will happen, but the death of them will never *be* them.

That story, that they are liberating themselves, that they are going to get there in the future, relaxes them. It makes that sense of not feeling loved and abandoned feel better, it feels less strong. That's all it's doing. But if that body is destined for the "me" to drop away, then it will happen despite them doing it or not doing it. It happens on its own. It's not somebody's doing, but they might have to dream the whole time that they are doing it. That might be something that has to happen, but it's not them doing anything. There is no one in there doing anything, there is just doing happening.

Actually, there is nothing happening, really.

Q: *What do you mean when you say that, that there is nothing happening?*

Lisa: There are no things, are there? There are just energies expressing themselves, there are no **actual** things. Only things in description, in language. If everything is changing, then there *is* no thing. There is nothing happening, which means there is Oneness.

Q: *Thank you very much.*

Lisa: Thank you, I enjoyed talking with you.

One Flow

Q: *I wanted to thank you for your response to my e-mail. It was so helpful. Whatever you have going there, I want what you're having.*

Lisa: You already have it. I *am* you.

Q: *Yeah, just trying to get the mind to realize that, I guess.*

Lisa: It's not the mind that will realize it. It's your nature. It's the mind that obstructs things. The original I is your nature. It's just that the mind divides everything and makes it seem like your true nature is "out there."

Q: *Would you say that nature is covered up like layers of an onion?*

Lisa: Yeah. If you put a blue filter on a light, it's still the same light but it gives the appearance of being blue. The nature of everything is always free, and you *are* everything. The filter gives the appearance of self and other.

Q: *The last couple of days some interesting things have been happening. I don't know what to make of it. It has nothing to do with meditation or concentration or anything, I just kind of woke up one morning and there was no suffering, continuously, for like a whole day. It's starting to fluctuate now, but there have been extended periods where things are just happening, just like what you talk about.*

Lisa: Nice. You can't make it happen, and it becomes so obvious that it is not your doing. It just happens and it just disappears. It's not you having any control. It's just happening.

Q: *Up until this point, it's all been about pain or pleasure, and by that I mean indulging in pleasure and pushing away pain. This had nothing to do with that. Not much actually changed. Everything was normal, but situations that would have aggravated me at work just didn't.*

Lisa: You could call it peace, but it's not really, because that's a state. It's just the absence of something that you can't really name or hold on to. It's just an absence of this something that is making something stick.

Q: *Right. It wasn't like Samadhi or Bliss. It was just really interesting, because it's not what I would have thought at all.*

Lisa: Well we may not be talking about the same thing, we don't know. But the thing that is great about what u said is that there is no suffering, so there is no longing for something else, for something to be different. It's absolutely what is wanted, but just not in the way that you would think. It is as you wanted because nothing is there trying to get to something else.

Q: *I would say however, that doing Vipassana totally had something to do with it. I don't think that without Vipassana the awareness would have been there to allow that to happen. Do you have anything to say about that?*

Lisa: Can the experience of doing Vipassana be separate from the Big Bang? Can it be separate from going to school? Can it be separate from you buying your first car or falling over and cutting your knee? It's all one movement happening, so how can you separate Vipassana out more?

Q: *I see what you're saying, and I agree. Do you think that there is a purpose for it only to realize there is no purpose?*

Lisa: No, I think it's all just one flow happening, and it can happen in Vipassana or not doing Vipassana. *In* that story, Vipassana was part of it. Vipassana can't be separated out, and that includes the person that went to prison for paedophilia and the stars at night.

The mind is highlighting one particular element because that seemed to have a profound effect. There is nothing that is more God or more Divine. It took you identifying with your brother, or your sister bullying you, or being an only child. It took your parents being a particular way. All of it is relevant.

Have you ever considered writing a play or a book? Are you creative in any way like that?

Q: *Yeah, I'm a musician.*

Lisa: Okay, so then you know that every note that comes is divinity because of all the notes before. In listening to music, where is the most divine note? Where is the most important note? To hear the most beautiful bit in a song, it's taken all the notes before to make it most beautiful.

I used to be a playwright, and that's why I brought it up. It was obvious when I was writing plays. It became obvious that there could never be any separation out of the story. If I wrote a bad character or the baddie, you could see how every action that came before led to that bad action. It is the same with the goodie, and there was no separation in it.

It is so beautiful when it begins to be seen that there is no separate thing happening. This is absolute *Love*. In Buddhism they used to say that the cart cannot be before the horse, and you basically begin to see that no action can ever be separate.

Q: *This is challenging me big-time, and I think that's a good thing.*

Lisa: Yeah, because we want to live in these cut-off stories, and if we live in cut-off stories, we will find separation. When you see that the body-mind mechanisms that taught you the identification of you are no different from the ones that taught you the un-identification, it's all one movement. They are not separate and they can't come without each other.

Q: *I see what you're saying. I guess I have to sit with this. I have one more question for you: the old Lisa, the ego-centred self, she practiced, right?*

Lisa: Yes, I did, but not latterly; latterly she realized she was screwed. But yes, when I was younger I was a practicing Buddhist for five years.

Q: *Probably forms of yoga as well, right?*

Lisa: No, not really. I would much rather just sit there with my eyes closed. The personality of Lisa is a bit lazy when it comes to physical exercise. Latterly there was a really big comprehension of how screwed Lisa was, like screwed in the sense that she couldn't be separate from everything else that was happening. Therefore, there was no independent act that she could find to get her to liberation. Liberation was the movement of things, it wasn't an individual thing.

Q: *That ten-day course that I took really set me on fire!*

Lisa: But it took everything that led up to that ten-day retreat to set it on fire. The mind wants to separate it out because then it can have a hero of Vipassana.

Q: *I think that from everything you have said, and what I am gathering, I was trying to glorify that experience. But the point of that peak experience is to be let go of.*

Lisa: Exactly. That's really beautiful. That's what the mind is always doing; it's trying to hold things up as superhero or the devil. When it sees those stories that say, 'This is how I got here and you can get here if you do that.' it begins to dissolve. Then it begins to be left with a lot more 'I don't know.'

Q: *It's a mind-fuck.*

Lisa: Yeah, but it's so beautiful. ~

Other

Q: *Who is another person?*

Lisa: If you don't see yourself, and there is not a "me" dynamic appearing, then you cannot see another. Who is another person? Who is your wife or husband or friend? When that functioning of "you" stops, everybody else stops.

Q: *So what is the "other" for you then?*

Lisa: There's nobody there. It can be a difficult thing to talk about. Who you see is only projection, a projection of that "me" story. If you don't think, you don't see another. I'm not saying this is about thinking or not thinking. I'm simply trying to point to the emptiness of everything. It can be quite scary really.

Unless a body-mind expresses a problem, I don't see a problem. I don't even see you, there is only movement happening. It's absolutely liberating because you are no longer seeing yourself everywhere, or a self in relationship with people.

All suffering comes from you being in relationship with people. This you that is in relationship with another is so heavy and full of mental activity of what the other has done to you, or what you are doing to them.

There is no other, there is movement seemingly happening. There is also no movement happening and it is absolute stillness.

This is so important. Who is it that you are seeing? I'm not saying that you become passive. You're probably wondering how then do you act? I am talking about the impersonality of life. There is no person in anything. There is no individual free will in anyone.

All suffering arises from the dynamic that says 'I am a somebody acting separately from you.' It is rather funny that that assumption is being made, because how is that possible? How can we ever find the start and stop to anything? When did the body's actions start happening? When you woke up this morning, or was it when your mother told you to be good? Was it when you were born or when your mom and dad made love?

This whole story that says I am acting and they are acting, I'm right and you're wrong, this whole energy is what the mind thrives on. What I am talking about may seem incredibly scary because it is the absolute end of control or thinking you have control. The "me" is always telling the story that if I am not in control, then chaos is going to happen. This here is chaos, everything is going to die. This is a world of growth and death. This is absolute freedom, but really what has to be confronted is 'who is the other?'

I assure you that the mind wants to stay in blame. It wants to stay in the idea that "I" have done wrong, and "they" have done wrong.

As the energy stops focusing on free will, then it will be seen that there is no separation, that this is life happening and it is absolutely free.

The flow of life is brutal and beautiful at the same time. There is constant growth and destruction, birth and death. Freedom cannot therefore be found in the flow of life, but it can be found in the stillness, which is always here. ~

Who Cares?

Q: *How do I know when I am done?*

Lisa: You won't. The "you" won't give a care anymore. The "you" there will collapse and stop looking at itself, and it will just be what is happening. There can be many highs and lots of experiences as the person collapses, and often the mind will conclude that it is done now or **this** is it. Who is it that is concluding that?

Q: *It's a thought that arises.*

Lisa: And that thought is still believed in, right?

Q: *No, it's not really believed in, no.*

Lisa: It still thinks it's somewhere. It still thinks it is somewhere in an experience. This is what is getting deconstructed, but it has nothing to do with you or me. In non-duality there can be a collapse of that one that is taking life personally and feels like life is happening to them.

Q: *You know from direct knowledge?*

Lisa: What is direct knowledge?

Q: *From your experience.*

Lisa: Is that direct knowledge? How many times have you lied about your own experience? Can you ever talk about your own experience? If you're in a good mood, the experience will look different than when you're in a more negative or bad mood. The story will change depending on what veils are up. You just don't know. All I can say is that the one that cares collapses, then it's just *this*. It's not looking at itself or questioning where it is on the spiritual path. It is just a big question mark where nothing is being held onto as you.

It has nothing to do with you; it's not you doing it.

Q: *I think you have answered my question. Thank you.*

Lisa: Thank you. ~

Money

Q: *I don't resonate with any kind of job. Any thoughts on that?*

Lisa: (Laughter) I like that, 'I don't resonate with any kind of job.' You could survive without a job in this country. The conditions may not be very pleasant, but you can survive without a job.

Money and Love are suffered over the most in the "me" dynamic. The money represents fear and death and not being able to physically maintain the body. It also represents status and position in society, as well as joy and pain. The money issue has such a huge role in the personal "me" dynamic. The whole notion of money is a made-up notion as it is something that the humans had to imagine and then trade in this imaginary form.

We give notes or these round coins in different shapes in order to trade. Money has zero value really, only the value that society gives to it. Money comes with such great insecurity in that one's safety is dependent upon producing enough of these notes and coins. My sense of position in society is based on how many of those notes and coins I can get together and trade in order to have really good items.

That momentum that has always taken responsibility for money, that "me" dynamic that has taken personal responsibility for money, is not the one that is controlling money. It really feels like that "me" dynamic is controlling money. But that "me" dynamic is a creation, not the creator. You have never earned money, you have never got yourself a job, you've never lived your life, you never earned your car. You have never done any of that.

The "me" dynamic that is saying 'I've got to get a job, I've got to get more money, I've got to pay my rent, I've got to increase the bank balance.' was **never** the creator.

That's full-on!

It really feels like that dynamic was the creator, like you were controlling your life. That very dynamic is a creation, or an appearance, just like the appearance of money or light or sound. Within that personal dynamic is an apparent thinker saying, 'I am choosing, I am earning my money, I am the one that has kept my bank balance above zero.' It gives the appearance of there being a someone, but it wasn't the chooser. It's a creation, just like everything else. Isn't that fantastic? You never have to earn your money; the "me" dynamic never has to earn its money. The "me" is most probably saying 'No, everything else, that's okay, but I have to earn money. I have to earn money and get myself a job. I have to look for a job and I have to be nice to my boss.' That's all an appearance.

The "me" is not the creator. That chucks everything on its head! All that stress at night, or the waking up in the middle of the night and feeling stressed about it, and the worrying about how you're going to produce it, was just a game, never the actuality. The "me" is then more than likely going to start to say something like 'Yes, but I need lots of money because I need a good story.'

So to answer your question, at the moment no jobs are happening, so more than likely no money is happening. I assure you that it is highly unlikely that your body is going to starve to death. It might be completely broke and poor, but that is only in a description. Nothing is ever poor or has a lack of money. You never have money anyway because money is only an imagination. It's all a game in a dreamland.

Maybe the real problem here is not that there is no job to resonate with, or not having money. The problem comes from the one that thinks that it's in control and it needs to make things different. It needs to make life different and needs to live up to what it thinks life **should** be. 'I shouldn't be starving and I shouldn't be homeless.' This is absolute free-fall into nothing, an absolute loss of that controller.

This is freedom. *This* is the Peace which is looked for. It's never **in** the money.

This is outrageous for that personal "me" dynamic to hear. I assure you, it *is* what is looked for. A large bank balance is not what is looked for. What is looked for is an absolute not knowing and life appearing without that one that thinks it knows life or is in control of life.

Q: *So are you saying that a job will happen if it happens?*

Lisa: Yeah, the job will happen or not, depending on whether the momentum to get a job or not get a job will happen.

That's the way it's always been. You never were in control of your life. The you is a creation, a dance or a game. That one that thinks it was controlling never got you a job, and it never got you the money. It was just another appearance happening. So yes, a job will happen or it won't. All that worry or anxiety over it is just a game that life is playing, a drama that life is acting out. There is no vulnerability. There is only vulnerability in stories.

Everything dies, all things are constantly changing. There is no freedom in trying to preserve anything. That's just fighting what *is*.

Q: *So does that mean that there is no responsibility?*

Lisa: Yes, that is what it means. There is no responsibility. Responsibility is a dream, a waking dream. ~

a sensual curl
a dark wave
intimate as a lover's touch
see on its surface
reflections of a pier
which the water is gradually wearing down
the wave rises out of some unknown depth
there is no hint of how the story will end
but it is already written

~Stream Ohrstrom

Claiming

Q: *When there is no "me" left, can there be love for your partner?*

Lisa: You won't see a partner anymore, and that is so strange to say. The body could be with another body most of the time, but you won't see them as your partner. The body could be saying 'I love you, you're fantastic.' but there is not someone in there that is saying that or claiming that. ~

Loss

Q: *Can you expand on love being complete loss?*

Lisa: The personal entity, that dreamed entity or energetic contraction, is always trying to hold on to things. It believes that it is a body and takes itself to be a thing. There is no solid thing, nothing. Everything is moving, and there is no one solid thing. You can't ever have one solid body. Drinking water happens, and then disappears and becomes body. The skin is always falling off. It's all energy. When you get down into it, it is all made of the same thing and it is constantly moving.

But the entity says: 'I am a body and I've got to make the body permanent.' and 'I've got to make other bodies permanent.' and 'I cannot lose any of that; that would be the worst thing, losing the body, losing the things, losing my story. I've got to make it solid; if I make it solid in some way, then I can have safety and I can control this. This person that I love so much that is standing in front of me, this dog, this car, this television that I love so much, I can keep them, I want to keep them, they are mine.'

There is no solid thing. It's always being lost and moving. The body is always moving into other objects. The entity is trying to hold on to something, and that is that suffering contraction that wants to keep it solid and permanent.

Love is loss. That is the natural way of things, they appear and disappear. There are never going to be separate things that stay still. They are always moving.

All the things are one thing, and this one thing is changing its appearance. As a child I can recall reading a quote that said, 'To know God is to live in a perpetual state of Loss.' I knew what that meant; I knew that that was the freedom. We think loss is negative, but it's love – true love. ~

Grief

Q: *Why does it still hurt so much and for so long after my sister died?*

Lisa: Because it does. Because that's what's happening. Why does the heart beat? Why is the sky blue? Why does none of this make any sense? Because that's the way it is.

We're always trying to get away from this rawness of experiencing; the sadness, the agony, the aching, but that's what *is*. That is part of what life is. It is set up to be in conflict. All forms die. Everything that comes into form changes into another form. That's part of it. It's brutal and it's sad, and it's happy and it's disastrous, and completely ordered.

This is what *is*, and whatever *is*, is. The "me" dynamic is always trying to go somewhere or get away from something. It can't get away from what is. It tries its very best, and in that trying more agony grows in longing for a better future. When? What is looked for is this, the rawness of experiencing.

There is no state of permanent bliss or ecstasy. There is no such thing as not feeling sadness or pain. That isn't even what is wanted. What is wanted is experiencing, and experiencing is in opposites, beauty and ugliness, sadness and happiness, pain and pleasure.

These opposites are not separate; it's all one and the same thing. It's all God. Every last bit of it is God apparently experiencing itself through opposites. ~

Death

Q: *Once the body-mind mechanism dies, would you consider that as freedom or liberation as well?*

Lisa: Yeah.

Q: *Well, we don't really know what it is, I guess. It's a mystery, obviously.*

Lisa: It's a mystery, but it is kind of happening now. There is death happening now as well. There is a part of this where it is not even happening at all.

Q: *Whenever you say that, I get confused. Do you mean that everything arises and then it goes away out of nothingness? Is that what you mean?*

Lisa: Yes. There is an emptiness side to everything as well. There is every-thing and no-thing. The less clutter of "me" the more this becomes obvious. It's not something you see. It's a knowing, but not a knowing in thought.

I can't quite say how it is, but I can say that it is happening and it is not happening. It is quite obvious that physical death is the absolute freedom.

The personal entity dies and it is absolute liberation. ~

Bliss

Q: *A lot of the time it feels like Bliss is arising. It feels like a dissolving. I would say that I am gone, but I am not really gone because there is still kind of a human perspective. It feels really open and flowing, and it is very nice as the ego is not there. Also, there is another kind of experience that almost sounds like questioning, but it's like there is no human perspective anymore. This perspective is really like I strive to find a human perspective, it's like I'm from Mars or something. First I thought, 'Bliss is it,' but from the perspective of the other, then it's just an experience.*

Lisa: Bliss comes and goes. What is being talked about here is emptiness, a lack of something. That emptiness is full-on love because it is full. Bliss comes and goes, and you can't find who you are at all. Somebody may ask what the body has done, and the answer could be a description of the body and then it goes again to absolute emptiness.

Q: *But that also just comes and goes, the emptiness?*

Lisa: It's not that it comes and goes, it's that the person comes back and the person looks at it. You can't look at it when it's happening. When there is nobody there, you can't look at it, it's just full-on life happening. You can't even say it's full-on happening because maybe it's not happening.

There is nobody there that cares anymore. It's an absence **of** something that cares. It might be that something comes back, and it might be very small. It is confusing because that person comes back and tells stories about it, and tries to organize and understand it. The "you" will never, ever get this. **Never**, ever. It's an absolute dissolving.

It can sometimes feel non-human because it's empty of a somebody. People were talking in the kitchen saying that it is the nicest thing that people have come to my talks, and I find it to be the oddest thing that people come to my talks. ~

Greed

Q: *There is a greediness, a wanting more of the taste or joyfulness that happens without thought.*

Lisa: Yes, but what it comes with is the absence of wanting to cling to it. I understand the word greediness. I can go with that, but there is not somebody there that is making it continuous. There is not a sense of clinging to it because it is heaven or love. It's the absence of somebody that could hold onto that because love is free, which means that it is in constant loss.

It's like magic, this world. That energy of that person is saying, 'Please, let me hold on to something.' Love, is the loss of it all. So it's like, 'Please, just my children.' It's so sad sometimes. 'Just my dog.' 'Okay then, just the money. I'll take the money.'

Nothing is left; it's a world of constant disappearance. The energy that is trying to hold on to it can be so playful and it can also be so sad. It can be so playful in finding the lover, saying 'This is it.' The lover can be the most exciting, when the personal is still there and you think you find the *one*, and *have* them in some way, that you two are a team and can be together. That can be incredibly pleasurable. But then there is the other side to that; you can lose them. ~

Banana Fritters

Q: *How did this shift happen with you? How did that "me" dynamic disappear?*

Lisa: What dies in awakening is the dream that you were ever awakening, and that you had experiences of awakening. Who do you imagine this Lisa to be? The only person that we can ever talk about is somebody in time. Time always arises here in Alive-ness, time is not the actual reality. The mind is absolutely fixated with who it is in time.

What seemingly happened was that there was a moment in Bali, where suddenly the energy of Alive-ness or Being-ness was no longer bound to a story in time, or bound to a body. It collapsed.

At first there was an interest in talking about it, but that too disappeared and became another story.

It was in Bali and I was eating banana fritters. ~

You Don't Have a Life

Q: *Lisa, yesterday I had a lot of resistance after satsang. When you were talking about these life patterns and not being able to change them, in my head there were all of these things being said like 'Of course you can change.' My mind the whole time was arguing with you, and I felt this energetic pull inward, this contraction the whole day.*

Then we went to Arunachula and it dropped and went away, and then it came back. In the night at five, it started again, 'It's not true, of course you can change the patterns, I can do something. She can do something.' Then suddenly I realized that I am always thinking that I have a life, and then you say you don't have a life and I don't want to hear that but please will you tell me again?

Lisa: Because if change is going to happen, it requires thought or that energy to come up for that change to happen. And maybe there is a belief that you are creating that energy or that thought to come up to change that. Where does that thought and that energy come from? Is there a "you" in there creating that thought, or does it suddenly appear and then action happens or no action happens?

Q: *There is such a strong belief that I do it, that she can do something about it.*

Lisa: Yes, and say if you see someone suffering and they never change anything, then the thoughts might go to, 'They never change. They could do something if they wanted to, but they don't.' It requires both energy and thought. The question is, where does that energy and thought to change come from? Where is that coming from?

When it is seen that there is absolutely no person in there doing that, that it is coming from absolute empty space, then it is seen that nobody ever did anything. Who you thought you were was just thoughts and sensations and energies appearing, giving the impression that there is somebody there doing.

It's terrible for the one that thinks it is doing. In another way it is absolute relief and the end of blame, because then you can never blame again someone for not doing something. When it is seen that there is absolutely no one creating these energies and thoughts, then there is no longer blame. Blame and guilt are the majority of the suffering. That is the majority of the time what the contraction is, 'They could have done something different, I should have done something different.'

When it is seen that all of it is coming from absolute empty space, from no-one, then you see that no-one ever did anything wrong. The source or the root of all thoughts and feelings come from absolute emptiness. Well, actually they don't really come from it – that's just a figure of speech. They *are* it.

It's not that doing stops. I know that you are a masseuse, you never did that either.

Q: *Yes, I am a therapeutic masseuse and this was always my question. Sometimes they come once and there is healing, and sometimes they come twenty or thirty sessions and they don't change, nothing happens. I've always wondered why. I don't know where it is that change happens.*

Lisa: This may sound dry but it's not. Life decides healing or not. It's not that your massage or healing practice is useless, it's just not the source. It's part of the flow. In the past you may have thought that *"it"* was doing something. *It* is an absolute divine expression of Oneness now expressing itself in healing, in massage. There is nothing wrong with that. Sixty or seventy percent of the people might come and find that pain has fallen away. It is never because of the massage. It is because life is expressing itself in that way. It's not to say that this is the end of massage, it is the end of the belief that you are doing it. *This* is a beautiful expression.

Often people hear this message and they think I'm saying don't do whatever it is that you think is useful. What I am talking about is the activity of mind that is putting importance on something they are doing, falls away. The mind wants to make sense of this, but really what it is trying to do is make safety and a position as to where they fit into the world. We simply can't know. We are just instruments of life, playing out the role. The mind wants the safety and it wants to keep the idea that there is more in the future. ~

When I was the Forest.

*When I was the stream, when I was the
forest, when I was still the field,
when I was every hoof, foot
fin and wing, when I
was the sky
itself,*

*no one ever asked me did I have a purpose, no one ever
wondered was there anything I might need,
for there was nothing
I could not
love*

*It was when I left all we once were that
the agony began, the fear and questions came,
and I wept, I wept, And tears
I had never known
before.*

*So I returned to the river, I returned to
the mountains. I asked for their hand in marriage again,
I begged – I begged to wed every object
and creature,*

*and when they accepted,
God was ever present in my arms.
And he did not say,
'where have you
been?'*

*for then I knew my soul – every soul –
has always held him.*

Meister Eckhart

Many thanks to

Julie Rumbarger, Paul Smit, Melissa Lee Schwartz,
Veronica Cairns, James Cairns, Ron Cairns, Khaleesie,
Laurent Levy, Roger Castillo, Vicky Parsons,
The Foundation of the Western Buddhist Order,
Yvonne Renshaw, Greg Frampton.

All rights reserved. No part of this book
may be reproduced, stored in a retrieval system,
or transmitted by any means, electronic, mechanical,
photocopying, recording, or otherwise, without the
express written permission of both Lisa Cairns
and Julie Rumbarger.

Preface and Story by Lisa Cairns.

Made in the USA
Monee, IL
10 June 2021